TEACHING FRENCH

TEACHING FRENCH

An Introduction to Applied Linguistics

ROBERT L. POLITZER
Stanford University

Second Edition

John Wiley and Sons, Inc.

New York London Sydney Toronto

Charles Staubach, *University of Arizona*

CONSULTING EDITOR

ISBN 0 471 00430 8
Library of Congress Catalog Card Number: 65-14561
Printed in the United States of America

10 9 8 7 6 5

Foreword

This book deals with the teaching of French—primarily the imparting of the basic skills at the high school or college levels. It is a textbook on the application of linguistics, with heavy emphasis on application. I feel that the language teacher, primarily concerned with concrete problems facing him in his language classes, is not likely to pursue in detail the study of the rather refined and exacting science of language, unless he is first made aware of the possible contribution of this study to the solution of teaching problems. The first part of this book is, therefore, devoted entirely to general methodological considerations. In the second part linguistic concepts are introduced, but the emphasis remains on the teaching of French rather than its scientific analysis. It is my hope that many teachers will want to pursue the science of language more deeply and in greater detail than it has been dealt with in this book. The connections between language teaching and linguistics are varied and subtle; further study of linguistics will prove for language teachers a rewarding experience in terms of their teaching skills and competency.

The aim of this book is not to teach French, but to show how to teach French on the basis of linguistic knowledge; the reader is presumed to have a mastery of the French language and the book aims to develop in the reader an awareness of the pattern conflicts between French and English and the remedies which a "linguistic" teaching method can offer. I fervently hope that I have avoided the pitfall of describing the already familiar facts of the French language under the guise of a new and different terminology. I also feel that this book supplements rather than duplicates various other pedagogical and linguistic works which have either appeared recently or are about to appear in the near future (more technical works on applied linguistics, or laboratory methodology, the exhaustive French–English contrast analysis currently in preparation by the Modern Language Association's Center of Applied Linguistics).

I acknowledge gratefully the help given by Mr. Michio Hagiwara of the University of Michigan in preparing the manuscript of the first edition for publication and in offering suggestions which have led to substantial modification of the original text. My special thanks go to my friend, Prof. Charles N. Staubach, co-author of the Spanish companion volume of this work, for his invaluable assistance and for providing corrections and improvements which were utilized in the second edition of this work. I am very grateful indeed for the criticisms and many encouraging comments received from my fellow linguists and French teachers. I trust that they will continue to let me have the benefit of their reactions and experience.

RLP

Stanford University,
March, 1964.

Contents

PART ONE

CHAPTER I

The Meaning of "Applied Linguistics"

There is, or at least there ought to be, a very intimate relationship between linguistics—the scientific study of languages—and language teaching. Yet the exact nature of this relationship seems to be disputed; some language teachers, especially those coming from the linguistic camp, see in linguistics and its application to language teaching the answer to all the problems that have ever confronted the language teacher; others feel that linguistics contributes nothing except a new jargon that can change little, if anything, in the language teaching situation. For others, holding less extreme points of view, the application of linguistics to language teaching means primarily an emphasis on an audio-lingual ("aural-oral") approach, or the use of the language laboratory, or classes taught by native informants, or the "Mimmem" method, which consists primarily of the student's mimicking sentences uttered by the instructor.

It seems therefore appropriate to the author to summarize very briefly what he considers to be the most important contributions of linguistics to language teaching. These contributions concern two phases of language instruction: the preparation of teaching materials and the actual presentation and drill of teaching materials in the classroom and the laboratory.

The contributions to the preparation of teaching materials are:

(1) By comparing the linguistic analysis of the native language of the learner—in our case English—with that of the language to be studied —in our case French—we highlight the major difficulties encountered by the learner. This comparison enables us, therefore, to construct

1

teaching and testing materials quite systematically and to give due emphasis to the points of real difficulty.

(2)   Linguistic analysis may enable us to describe the language to be learned more simply or economically than is done in conventional grammars. This simplification, in turn, will facilitate the task of the learner.

(3)   Linguists are primarily interested in *spoken* language and see in written forms only a secondary representation of the spoken word. Linguistic analysis will furnish rules of the spoken language which are often simpler than (or at any rate different from) the rules of the written language which are given in many traditional grammars. There are various advantages for the teacher in being able to formulate rules concerning the spoken language; obviously these are the only rules that can properly be used in the planning of the purely "audio-lingual" phase of any course, and even if writing and orthography go hand in hand with speaking, students should be aware of their behavior in speech as well as in writing.

In the area of actual classroom practice linguistics has made two major contributions:

(1)   Linguists have realized that language is behavior and that behavior can be learned only by inducing the student to behave—in other words to perform in the language. Thus, linguists distinguish rather unanimously the learning of language (performing in the language) from the learning of rules and grammatical terminology. This does not necessarily imply that rules and grammatical terminology are superfluous and can be dispensed with altogether. But prescription and description cannot take the place of language learning itself.

(2)   Linguistic analysis gives an excellent clue as to what units of behavior should be taught in individual exercises. Linguistic analysis is basically a way of decomposing utterances of a language into their component elements until the linguist obtains the entire inventory of building stones which the speaker of the language has at his disposal in order to construct those utterances. Language learning as viewed by the linguist is in a sense the direct application of this process of analysis. The learner gets to know slowly, systematically, and one by one each one of those building stones that have been identified and analyzed by the linguist.

Applied Linguistics is then that part of linguistic science which has a direct bearing on the planning and presentation of teaching material. This means that Applied Linguistics is primarily connected with that branch of linguistic science which deals with the description and analysis of current contemporary languages, synchronic or descriptive linguistics. This does not mean that the other main branch of linguistics, historical linguistics, is completely unrelated to language teaching. Historical or diachronic linguistics is important insofar as it helps in understanding the present state of affairs. Only historical linguistics can provide a meaningful answer to the question *why*, which is so often asked by our students: Why are certain verbs irregular? Why are there two sets of pronouns in French? The answers can only be given in terms of the history of the language. This means that the teacher should have a grasp of the essentials of that history. Yet, at the same time, historical linguistics does not have the same immediate bearing on teaching that descriptive linguistics has. As a matter of fact, too much historical explanation or the confusion of historical statements with those describing the present state of affairs, will only bewilder and confuse the student.

One point should be made clear from the very outset: Linguistics or Applied Linguistics as such has no answer to many of the problems which are still confronting the language teacher; in other words Applied Linguistics will not help us in designing "the method" with which we can achieve fluency in a language after two years of High School work. Applied Linguistics does not tell us how to teach effectively in overcrowded classrooms nor will it lead to the preparation of teaching materials which can be used efficiently on students of widely varying intelligence and ability in the same classroom. Linguistic science as such has no direct answer when it comes to some of the purely psychological factors in language learning, such as motivation and attitudes on the part of the student; nor should it be expected in a language as well known and studied as French, that the application of linguistics will lead to major new discoveries concerning the basic facts of the language. True enough, linguistic analysis of current French speech may bring our ideas on French somewhat more up-to-date or may lead to a more accurate description of such elusive features as intonation and stress. This is, however, not the major contribution of linguistics to teaching.

To repeat, the major contribution lies in the systematic comparison of English and French and the application of a teaching methodology which, through systematic drills, attempts to build up the student's knowledge of the structure of the foreign language, while at the same time eliminating those errors which are caused by the patterns of the student's native English. It is primarily to the demonstration of these aspects of Applied Linguistics that this book will be devoted.

CHAPTER II

A Linguistic Teaching Method?

Some linguists have taken the point of view that there is no such thing as a linguistic teaching method; linguistics as the study of language deals with the subject matter to be taught in a language course, not with the teaching method to be employed. Strictly speaking, this is true; yet at the same time, the very basic facts concerning the very nature of language seem to endorse some and contradict others of the currently employed methods of teaching.

A **language** may be defined as **the system of arbitrary** (vocal) **symbols by means of which the members of a speech community communicate with each other.** The word arbitrary in the above definition is in need of some further explanation. It implies that normally at least there is no intrinsic and necessary connection between the symbols and the concepts for which they are used. Exceptions to this normal state of affairs are, for instance, onomatopoetic words, i.e., calling a dog a "bow-wow" in imitation of the noise made by the animal. But usually the "reason" for any symbol or construction in language lies not in what is to be expressed, but in (1) the history of the language and (2) the system of the language itself. In other words, a Frenchman calls a cat *chat* not because *chat* seems to be the sequence of sounds particularly suited to refer to a cat but because (1) the word evolved from a late Latin word *cattus* which is the ancestor or "reason" for Modern French *chat*, (2) and if a Frenchman changed all or only one of the sounds of the word *chat* (let us say to *rat*), he would no longer be understood as referring to a cat: *chat* is what is required by the system of the French language.

5

The fact that language is a system in which every particle receives its value from the total complex in which it functions is all-important. Perhaps an analogy may help to elucidate this point. Let us think of a linguistic system as a set of building stones that are available, again and again, to every speaker of the language, in order to build the "bridge of communication" between himself and others. A speaker of French is asked: *Où est votre livre?* Quickly he turns to the set available to him and answers:

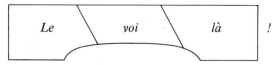

A speaker of English in the same situation might have answered:

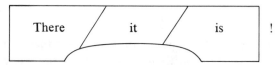

To pursue our analogy: the French and the English bridges are the same insofar as they fulfill the same purpose. The French and English utterances have the same meaning but the individual building stones of French have absolutely no relation to those of English. Their shape, the very possibility of fitting them into this particular bridge was determined entirely by the French set from which they were taken and the same was true in turn about the English building stones.

A great many—perhaps most—of the mistakes made by a learner of a foreign language are due to one simple and comprehensible failure: the learner mistakenly equates building stones of the foreign system with individual building stones of his system. He wants to use the foreign building stones as if they had been taken from his own set.

Now it is perfectly true that there are many constructions in which two languages parallel each other. These constructions are responsible for the errors of the students. They are a blessing in one way because they are easy in themselves; they are a curse because they establish that mistaken identification of building stones of different systems. Certainly

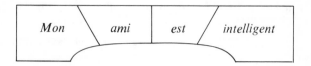

corresponds very nicely to

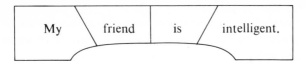

But it is also that type of construction which is indirectly responsible for such an impossible construction ("fractured French") as, let us say:

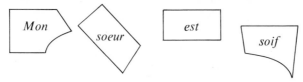

The fundamental lesson that every language student has to learn is simply that elements of one language cannot be equated with those of another language. Dictionaries are a necessary evil, of course; and good dictionaries try to remedy the evil as much as possible by supplementing the correspondences of isolated words with sample sentences demonstrating how the foreign word, or the foreign building stone actually fits into a construction. But the simple fact that building stones of language systems do not correspond to each other discredits any teaching method which attempts to present the foreign language precisely in terms of such correspondences. A student should never learn isolated words, isolated building blocks. He must learn complete constructions, he must learn how the individual building stones fit together. Only that will enable him to avoid producing fractured French.

In connection with this, one word concerning linguistics and the "grammar translation" method: many teachers have said with some concern that they felt that some of the new linguistic methods seem to neglect the teaching of grammar. I, for one, have never seen how a linguistic approach to teaching could possibly dispense with an explicit or at least implicit grammatical analysis on the part of the student. The student must not only learn a construction, he must also realize how this construction is "made up," how it "comes apart," how some building stones can be replaced by others. From the linguistic point of view, the legitimate objections are not to the appropriate use of analysis or description as such, but rather (1) to the substitution of the learning of grammatical terminology and rules for the learning of the constructions themselves, which is a *misuse* of grammar; and (2) to the idea that the grammatical analysis of a construction in the native language, in our case English, should be the basis for translation into the foreign language.

The latter idea can be best demonstrated at its probable source, the traditional process of translating English into Greek or Latin. Take an English sentence like

The father sees the boy.

Conventional grammatical analysis applied to this sentence shows that it is composed of a subject, verb, and direct object:

subject	verb	direct object

The subject, father, is identified as the nominative of a noun, the verb as a third person singular present, the direct object as the accusative of a noun:

nominative	third person sing. verb	accusative

With this information the student is now able to put the English sentence into Latin:

Pater	*videt*	*puerum.*

There are various theoretical and practical objections to this teaching approach. On the theoretical side this approach presupposes the idea of some sort of universal grammar: the English sentence is analyzed and transformed into a sort of disembodied ghost construction—subject + verb + object—which is given a concrete body again in another language. The underlying grammatical analysis is presumably equally valid for both languages. But in our sample sentence the analysis was possible only because we analyzed the English sentence in terms of a grammar which was imported from Latin in the first place. Nominative and accusative, terms which refer to a declensional system of nouns with specific declensional endings, make good sense in Latin, but they do not mean much for a language like English in which nouns are no longer inflected. Note, incidentally, that the process of going from English to Latin in terms of a "common grammar" not only required a latinized grammatical analysis of English, but also that the translation we obtained, *Pater videt puerum*, presented a slight anglicization of

Latin; for the word order **subject** + **verb** + **object** is highly unusual in Latin. *Pater puerum videt* would have been a better answer. The translation process going through the medium of a presumably universal grammar somewhat obscured the specific characters of either language: in this case the fact that in English the subject-object relationship is expressed by word order, while in Latin it is signaled by case endings.

In the case of French, the lack of a "universal" grammar is perhaps less of an obstacle to the translation approach than it is in the case of Latin. In many ways English and French resemble each other more than English and Latin. Neither English nor French have declensional endings, and while French has more of a conjugational system than English (the -*s* of the third person singular is practically all that is left of the English conjugational endings), both languages rely largely on word order to express grammatical relationships: The father sees the boy and *Le père voit le garçon*, vs. The boy sees the father and *Le garçon voit le père*. To evolve a nonuniversal grammatical system which would fit both languages, in a majority of cases at least, does not seem too difficult. But I think that in the beginning French class the objection against the grammar translation method is not so much against the underlying theory, but rather against its practical results: (1) It forces the student to analyze and identify individual building stones in his own language first, which means that instead of learning complete constructions in French, he must arrive at the French constructions by learning sets of correspondences between English and French; (2) the constant cross-association between English and French leads (just because English and French are parallel in so many cases) to the assumption on the part of the student that they are parallel in many other cases, in which they are not; (3) all the cases in which English and French are not parallel must be presented as special problems or exceptions or idioms.

In a linguistic teaching approach, **the construction in the foreign language is the starting point of instruction.** The student learns how the construction is made up by exercises in which building stones are replaced by others. This shows him how the construction fits together and what the value of each building stone is. In a sentence like:

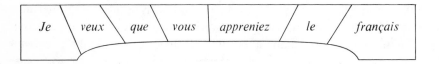

we show the student how *francais* can be replaced by *grec, latin,* et cetera, *appreniez* by *étudiiez, sachiez, compreniez,* et cetera, *veux* by *exige, doute,* et cetera. This teaches the student not only the fact that the building stones *appreniez, sachiez,* or *veux, exige,* belong to the same category since they can fit into the same spot of the construction, but it teaches also the construction, the "pattern" itself; for while we are replacing the individual elements of the construction by others, the construction itself, the "pattern," remains constant.

Another approach to the teaching of the use of a building stone is the comparison of two patterns which differ from each other only through the building stone or stones the student is supposed to learn. The comparison shows exactly how the new building stone fits into the pattern:

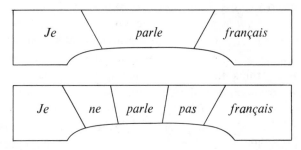

Again the student sees how the building stones fit into the pattern and he learns the value of the building stones by fitting them into a series of identical patterns:

Je cherche le livre   >   Je ne cherche pas le livre.
Je trouve le crayon   >   Je ne trouve pas le crayon.

The learning of constructions of patterns and the study of the value of building stones, through the process of transformation and substitution, are probably the cornerstones of the linguistic teaching approach. Most of the other "linguistic" teaching techniques to be discussed and illustrated later are basically adaptations of these two principles.

The advantages of these methods are that the student learns the constructions of the foreign language by processes which work from within the foreign language, not through translation from his native language, and that he learns them by observation and by speaking the foreign language, not by speaking about it. This does not mean that he should not learn rules, but that rules are primarily summaries of what the student is observing or doing. They are the descriptive statements about the language and they are, therefore, the description of the student's own performance. **Rules ought to be summaries of behavior.** They function only secondarily as predictors.

In conjunction with a drill in which, let us say, the student substitutes *j'ai peur, je crains, je me réjouis* into a construction like *je regrette que vous partiez*, it is certainly necessary to discuss the verbs which require the subjunctive and to point out the rules governing its use. But a rule like "The subjunctive is used in a subordinate clause after verbs of emotion"—even if it is a reasonably accurate predictor—will not establish by itself a behavior pattern that will lead the student to use the subjunctive correctly. The behavior is formed by actual performance in the language. The rule can reinforce the student's behavior, but it cannot establish it. We all know from our experience and that of our students how we can make certain mistakes in a foreign language again and again, even though we know perfectly well the rules governing the particular point in question.

The objection is sometimes raised that the "linguistic" teaching approach with its emphasis on the learning of complete patterns and oral performance contributes but little to the teaching methodology of a course in which reading knowledge is the primary goal. But here again several points can be made in favor of the learning of complete patterns and a certain amount of oral performance regardless of the ultimate objective. On the side of oral performance, it seems fairly clear that we make some sort of oral response—at least a silent one in form of lip movement—whenever we read. As long as there is such a response, we might as well make sure that it is a reasonably correct one. But perhaps the major argument in favor of the "linguistic" approach is the case for pattern learning. Unless the student learns to recognize complete patterns, his "reading" in the foreign language will in fact be a complicated, drawn-out and often erroneous process of deciphering. The identification of isolated building stones of the foreign languages with those of the native language is just as detrimental to effective reading as it is to effective speaking. Only after the major patterns, especially those in which French and English clash, have been learned through drill and pattern practice, should the student be made to read extensively on his own. The dictionary should then serve the purpose of filling in gaps in a pattern already recognized by the student, but just as in the process of learning to speak, it should not be used by the student to identify the individual elements in an attempt to assemble them into a meaningful whole. For example, a student faces a sentence like

Je veux lui cacher la vérité.

and with the help of a dictionary comes up with the translation

I want him to hide the truth.

This student should have received extensive drills in this particular pattern

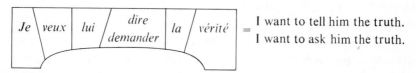

$=$ I want to tell him the truth.
I want to ask him the truth.

in contrast to

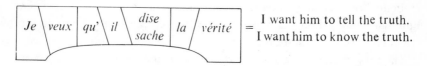

$=$ I want him to tell the truth.
I want him to know the truth.

before having been made to tackle this sentence. Pattern practice will help avoid fractured translations as well as fractured spoken French.

Pattern practice thus seems valid for the development of reading knowledge as well as for the teaching of production. Depending on the primary aim, the exact application will of course be different. In pattern practice for **production** the student must be given opportunity to actively produce the pattern, first through repetition and then in response to varied stimuli. Pattern practice for reading (in other words, practice in **instantaneous recognition of meaning**) takes a slightly different form. First of all, the continuous successive repetition of the same pattern seems less appropriate than it is in pattern practice for speaking: continuous repetition increases facility in production, but in fact distracts the learner's attention from the meaning of the pattern. Thus in pattern practice for reading, a spaced-out repetition which provides for reoccurrence of the same pattern appears to be more effective. Thus, if A^1 A^2 A^3, B^1 B^2 B^3, C^1 C^2 C^3 represent different examples of patterns A, B and C, a presentation of A^1 A^2 A^3 A^4, B^1 B^2 B^3 B^4, C^1 C^2 C^3 C^4 is necessary for teaching production, while a presentation of A^1 B^1 C^1, A^2 B^2 C^2, A^3 B^3 C^3, preferably in a meaningful context, will be more effective in focusing the student's attention on the meaning of the structures. In addition, pattern practice for recognition cannot, of course, consist merely of the student's repetition of the pattern, but must be an exercise that continually centers attention on the meaning of the pattern as it is encountered by the student. Thus in pattern practice for recognition, the patterns, in other words the grammatically essential elements, must be presented to the student in their entirety. The student's attention may be directed to them by asking him to provide substitution words within the pattern. The substitution words would of course have to be words which do not affect the grammatical meaning of the pattern as such—in other words, those whose meaning could probably be guessed from the context or looked up in the dictionary. A reading pattern exercise may thus take the form of a substitution exercise in which the student is asked to provide *any* meaningful replacement in sentences like: *Je ne crois pas que*_____*nous dise la*_____. *Je ne veux pas que*_____*vous accompagne au*_____. A somewhat similar approach, focusing on structure rather than on vocabulary, is taken by an apparently rather successful method which provides for possible recourse to interlinear translation for vocabulary items, while at the same time it withholds such translation for the elements essential for the recognition of grammatical relationships.

We have tried to show the difference between a linguistic approach and the grammar-translation method. Another question which is often asked by language teachers is: What about linguistics and the direct method? The answer is that the "direct method" is not necessarily in contradiction to a linguistic approach to teaching, though in fact it is incompatible with it in many cases. Linguistics as such cannot contribute significantly to the pedagogical decision of how the meaning of structures is to be supplied to the student.

Let us take the constructions:

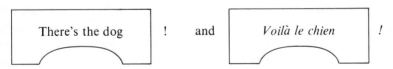

We can say that they mean the same thing because these are the constructions that a Frenchman and an Englishman would use in an actual situation, pointing at a dog. These sentences refer to the same thing, that is, they have the same **reference**. Now we can simply explain this to the student—ask him to accept the **total meaning** of the **total English sentence** as the equivalent of the meaning of the French sentence and then drill the French construction by substituting other nouns for *chien*; or we can actually produce the "reference" of the sentence in the classroom—point to a dog or at least the picture of a dog and say, *voilà le chien*, and then go on to other objects or pictures and say (making the student repeat), *voilà le cheval, voilà le tableau*, and so on. I believe that the important phase of this operation lies in the drill and not in the way in which the meaning of the sentence was supplied in the first place. Even if the explanation in English were avoided, there is, of course, a good chance that some students may have interpolated an English response between the picture and the *voilà le chien* of the teacher and may have translated the teacher's sentence. At the same time, it is likely that the avoidance of English will diminish the chance of a student's fracturing French by trying to establish the equation of French words with English words. Moreover, the approach through the object or the picture rather than through supplying the English equivalent may be important for sustaining the student's interest, especially, perhaps, at the elementary or junior high school level. A further important pedagogical advantage of the picture or object lies in the fact that it can provide a very economical nonverbal cue for a structure (not just a vocabulary item!) which the student has learned to associate with it. In other words, if the linguistic approach can be preserved and made compatible with the direct method, the latter seems to have an advantage over the explanation in English.

At the same time the very nature of the direct method makes it often very difficult to proceed according to a strictly linguistic organization of teaching materials. The linguist would like to organize his course and the presentation of the language according to the system, the structure of the language. He would like to add one by one the building stones of French, always going in minimal steps from one known construction to the next. The direct method channels a course into an organization which follows the patterns of the reality around us, the sequence of "events" rather than the structure of the language.

A typical early lesson in a direct methods course is apt to sound somewhat like this:

> *Je frappe à la porte. Je l'ouvre. J'entre dans la classe. Je m'assieds sur ma chaise. J'écris des notes dans mon carnet. Je me lève. Je commence à poser des questions aux étudiants.*

It is quite obvious that his "simple" lesson contains a variety of rather complex structures—some of them easy (*Je frappe à la porte*), and others of particular difficulty for the speakers of English (*Je pose des questions aux étudiants:* I ask the students questions). Strict adherence to the direct method makes it difficult to single out these difficult constructions for special drill and it makes it almost impossible to give grammatical explanations in the initial phases of the course. However, if the sentences used in the direct method lesson were based upon minimal structural steps, this problem would be eliminated, and the two methods made compatible.

This desirable fusion of methodologies appears to pose serious problems to writers of textbooks. Most of the "new-key" courses so far published revolve around dialogues to be memorized, dialogues which introduce vocabulary and constructions of a variety and complexity far beyond the level to be drilled or analyzed in the remainder of each corresponding unit. Any clearcut application of linguistic principles as outlined above is likely to be obscured where content becomes an overriding concern.

These, then, would seem the features that a teaching methodology has to follow in order to qualify as linguistically oriented:

(1) The starting point of any grammatical exercise is a complete construction in the foreign language.

(2) Special emphasis must be put on those elements of the foreign language which are made especially difficult by the interference coming from the native language.

(3) The actual learning of the foreign language takes place primarily by performance and habit-formation on the part of the student.

(4) Rules and grammatical explanation serve the purpose of describing to the student what he is doing and not of prescribing what he ought to do: constructions in the foreign language **must be learned as a whole rather than assembled.** At the same time, however, it should be emphasized that a linguistic teaching approach does in no way endorse or sanction the idea that a student should be ignorant of the grammatical structure of the patterns which he is learning.

(5) The presentation of teaching materials and the sequence of presentation is the one that is dictated by linguistic structure, and new building stones of the foreign language are learned one by one.

CHAPTER III

Some Psychological Aspects of Language Learning

The analyses and teaching procedures discussed in the following chapters are to a large extent the application of linguistic rather than psychological principles to the language learning area; but they are more than that, for linguistics does make certain psychological assumptions about languages, which in turn lead to psychological principles of language learning. Some of the more recent experiments and studies in the area of learning in general, and in language learning in particular, seem to bear out the validity of the principles of pattern drill, repetitions, et cetera, involved in the linguistic teaching approach. In this chapter, then, we shall explain briefly just what psychological assumptions, problems, and principles are involved in the linguistic approach to language teaching and its most important methodological adjunct: the language laboratory.

A complete review of learning theory and principle would go far beyond the scope of this text and it would not be very useful for our purpose. Much of modern psychology of learning is in itself controversial and debatable. Few of its principles—some derived from the observation of animals rather than humans—have been tested in their concrete application to language learning, although a number of promising studies have been undertaken in the last few years.

As a general framework for our psychological discussion it will be sufficient to keep in mind a few generally accepted principles: **by learning in the psychological sense, we understand an observable change in performance on the part of an individual.** Whether this change in performance is for the better or worse is not involved in the definition; one can "learn" arithmetic or French as much as one can "learn" bad table manners. The acquisition of the new habits of performance can be brought about in two distinct ways; either of the two involves the mechanisms of **stimulus** and **response**.

The first type of learning, called **classical conditioning**, involves what is called an associational shift. This process may be described, in a very oversimplified form, somewhat as follows: A piece of candy placed in the mouth serves as a stimulus (**S**) which produces salivation and a sense of pleasure as a reaction (**R**):

$$
\begin{array}{lcl}
\text{candy} & > & \text{pleasure} \\
\text{(physical stimulus)} & > & \text{(reaction)} \\
\textbf{S} & > & \textbf{R}
\end{array}
$$

The candy is now called by a name, "gum drop," which is repeated each time a piece of candy is presented. "Gum drop," a linguistic abstraction or symbol, is now associated with the physical object, candy, and becomes a participating or alternate factor with the original stimulus. We can denote this factor as **A**, and summarize the new situation thus:

$$
\begin{array}{lcll}
\text{candy} & + & \text{"gum drop"} & > \text{pleasure} \\
\text{(physical stimulus)} & + & \text{(name)} & > \text{(reaction)} \\
\textbf{S} & + & \textbf{A} & > \textbf{R}
\end{array}
$$

As a result of this association, we soon find that the word "gum drop" alone, in the absence of any actual candy, will produce salivation and what we might describe as an "echo" of sweetness and pleasure:

$$
\begin{array}{lcl}
\text{"gum drop"} & > & \text{pleasure} \\
\text{(name)} & > & \text{(reaction)} \\
\textbf{A} & > & \textbf{R}
\end{array}
$$

By the association of stimulus (**S**) with a substitute or alternate (**A**) we have **conditioned** the response mechanism or reaction (**R**), so that it will function even when the associational shift from $S > R$ to $A > R$ has been completed: the organism has been conditioned to react to a symbol even when the physical stimulus is not present.

In the learning of the mother tongue, **S** corresponds to the complex of stimuli created by a situation, and **A** represents the linguistic symbols —words, forms, and structures—with which the stimuli are constantly associated. So persistent is this process of association that the linguistic symbol, **A**, a substitute for reality **S**, comes to evoke whole complexes of responses or reactions **R**, and so to have **meaning**.

When the learning of a second language is undertaken, the process of associational shift cannot be repeated in this simple form. We do not refer here, however, to the simultaneous learning of two languages by a very young child in a bilingual environment, but to the acquisition of a new or foreign language by one who has already acquired the habits of his native tongue.

Much traditional methodology has focused the learner's attention on the association of elements of the new language, which we can designate as A^1, with those of the native speech, **A**. This gives us an additional substitution between **S**, the situation or external reality, and **R**, the response or meaning. Our formula would now be

$$S + A + A^1 > R.$$

The meaning (**R**) of the foreign language (A^1) is thus not one derived directly from the situational association. It is also identified with the meaning of the symbols of the native language. Our formulation, therefore, may become increasingly complex. For example,

$$S + {A \atop A^1} \updownarrow R \quad \text{or} \quad A \; S + A > R \atop A^1$$

It must be recognized that some association such as $A \leftrightarrow A^1$, appears to be inevitable. The learner invariably seeks the meaning of the foreign language by relating it to his own. This natural process leads, however, to serious interference in second-language learning. The first and more obvious form of interference is the painful necessity of translating to get at meaning, a slow and frustrating obstacle to communication, since it involves the interposition of an extra associational shift between stimulus and response. The more insidious form of interference is the intrusion of sounds, constructions, and meanings of the native language—all of which are matters of habit—into the patterns of the language being learned. This interference is the more difficult to combat because so little attention has been given heretofore to contrastive studies of pairs of languages.

"Mother tongue interference" is perhaps the most important psychological as well as linguistic consideration affecting our examination of methodologies. This concept will be constantly present in the rest of this book.

The second basic type of learning is called **instrumental**; in addition to an association of stimulus and response, it involves also the idea of the **reward** or satisfaction which the individual receives as the result of his performance. As we watch an infant or a small puppy beginning to react to sounds and sights in his environment, it appears quite plain that responses may at first be almost completely random; but a chance few of the responses result in the satisfaction of some desire, or the lessening of an anxiety. This satisfaction or reward becomes associated with the specific response after a number of chance occurrences, and thus serves to **reinforce** the learning of a particular response in answer to a particular stimulus.

In first-language learning, the child produces sounds at random, but certain configurations of sounds will win the approval of his parents or bring about certain results. The child is then communicating, and the reward will be his parents' attention. The response which brings reward will be learned. It is generally believed today that this process of chance and reinforcement is more fundamental in the very beginning of the infants' learning than is direct imitation of sounds and words modeled by the eager parent.

In second-language learning, of course, conscious imitation of sounds produced by the teacher becomes an important and obvious basis for identifying bits of new behavior to be learned. Nevertheless, the value of reward or reinforcement of correct responses to speed real control seems beyond the need for argument. Our problem will be to determine what teaching or learning devices are best calculated to provide for such reinforcement by reward or approval. We must observe carefully the way we use the term reward. A student may be anxious to get his homework done and be worried about not finishing it in time so that he can get to the baseball game. The response he produces in French, no matter how wrong, will find an immediate reward by his lessening of tension ("Thank God I'm done with the homework") and will thus be reinforced and learned. Our goal must be to control the learning of the student in such a way that reward of any kind is reserved only for correct responses.

Varying theories concerning the nature of learning lie behind the concepts of classical conditioning and instrumental learning, as well as other concepts we have not yet dealt with. The two most diametrically opposed views are those associated with behaviorism and those held by the "gestalt" psychologists.

In the behaviorist view, all learning results mechanically and automatically from stimuli and responses which are associated in the learning organism, and all learning is basically of this mechanical habit-formation type, and classical conditioning and reinforcement are the central mechanisms of all learning.

The other view, which is more flattering to our self-esteem and more popular with nonpsychologists, admits the role of habit formation but sees learning as more than that: the learner brings to the learning process his own creative ability to perceive and detect relationships, to appreciate patterns and configurations, to recognize analogies and contrasts. However much he may indeed be a mechanism shaped through stimuli or impressions received from the outside, he is at the same time an interacting organism, influencing the environment and conscious of at least a part of the processes in which he participates.

The linguist-pedagogue is forced to make a choice in the face of such conflicting views. For us, these views need not be mutually exclusive. Both kinds of learning seem to be involved as we analyze different parts of the complex processes of learning a foreign language. It will be seen in what follows that we recognize the importance of awareness and of the ability to abstract; the essential role of intellect is not at all denied, contrary to the erroneous interpretations of some defenders of older ideas. A natural concern for understanding must not blind us to the inevitable role of habit.

The psychology of second-language learning must take into account three important facts which inevitably determine much of the learning process. First, and perhaps most important, is that the native language interferes with the acquisition of the new one; second, that language is habit (or a complex of habits); and third, that language is an elaborate system. From the psychological point of view the problem of foreign language learning can perhaps be illustrated in the following way: A speaker of English is to learn the response *Robert est intelligent; Robert est stupide; Robert a chaud; Robert a froid*—all in the appropriate situations. One way of approaching the problem would be to teach all of the items involved separately as responses to specific stimuli (English sentences, pictures, et cetera). This learning process would be the safest; and also the most time-consuming. The other way would be to teach only *Robert est intelligent* and *Robert a chaud*. This approach would be more economical—only two responses have to be drilled instead of four. For *Robert est stupide* and *Robert a froid* we could rely on the student's ability to transfer; but it is obvious from the example that the reliance on **positive transfer** (*Robert est stupide* from *Robert est intelligent*) also invites the possibility of **negative transfer** or **interference** (*Robert "est" froid* rather than *Robert a froid*). Much of the discussion and confusion about teaching methodology, best age for learning, and so forth, simply stem from the fact that in language learning one can put the emphasis either on maximizing the learning by direct stimulus and response reaction and narrowing the area left to transfer—or on relying upon the individual's ability to transfer. I do not think that one can decide in absolute terms which approach to language learning is best: both have advantages and disadvantages. The first—minimizing the area left to transfer—implies by definition that more time must be spent on practice of individual examples of patterns, and that a large number of stimulus and response reaction must be provided for. The obvious advantage is that by narrowing the area left for transfer, we also cut down on the possibility of negative transfer or interference: the more practice, the fewer the mistakes. Reliance on transfer is more economical; but with transfer may also come negative transfer, so economy or efficiency on the one hand may on the other be exchanged for errors.

Yet no matter how large or small the area we want to leave to transfer, a certain number of correct responses must be learned in any case. This implies that they must be taught by producing the appropriate reactions to external stimuli. With respect to this response type of learning, it should be kept in mind that (1) a response can be learned only if it is performed; (2) a response is learned if it is rewarded; (3) rewarding of desired responses is by far more effective than the punishing of wrong ones; (4) the rewarding of desired responses is usually effective only if the reward is immediate rather than delayed.

The application of the above principles to teaching methodology is obvious. The important point is not to have the student "construct" correct or half-correct sentences. He must be made to produce a correct utterance. This may first take the form of repetition, but the correct utterance must be produced preferably in a situation in which it represents a response to a given stimulus, and thus satisfies the student's desire. This satisfaction may be the lessening of tension resulting from the student's answering the teacher's question, or it may be the satisfaction of pleasing the teacher or his own ego. Once the right response occurs, the teacher must let the student know immediately that the response was correct, so that the reinforcing effect of reward is exploited to the fullest degree.

It has been a well recognized principle among language teaching methodologists or educational psychologists that the real skill of the teacher lies not in correcting and punishing wrong responses but in creating situations in which the student is induced to respond correctly. Linguistic teaching methodology is basically just such a way of bringing the student into a situation in which wrong responses are impossible. In substitution and transformation exercises the possibility of error is small. Dealing with only one new element at a time also narrows down the possibility of gross errors.

Now let us consider the factor of transfer in language learning. We can communicate in our native language without apparent awareness of the nature of patterns, without the slightest notion of what the structure of our native language is like. We manipulate the structures mechanically and automatically. The goal of all language instruction is to achieve precisely the same kind of automatic control in the foreign language. We learn our first language through a staggering number of stimuli and responses, until the pattern is learned. But even learning the native language implies some sort of awareness of pattern and the ability to transfer patterns from one situation to another. The mere fact that small children will transfer "wrongly" or "negatively" even in their native language ("singed" for "sang") shows that transfer plays a rôle even in first language learning. At the same time, there is no danger of the pattern being interfered with by other firmly established patterns. Yet when we acquire a second language we can hope for an approximation of the process of learning the first language only if (1) we have a very large amount of time to learn the language, (2) we start the language at an age when our brain is still "plastic" enough to acquire new responses without much interference from others, (3) if we create a large number of situations in which the use of the second language is absolutely necessary. It is very unlikely that any of these conditions are fulfilled in a school or classroom. Even in the programs of teaching language in elementary schools the first condition we mentioned is normally not met.

All this points to the fact that in most second language learning situations the stimuli and responses should be arranged in such a way that they make the patterns of language clearly apparent to the student. This does not mean that the student needs to be able to "verbalize" about the patterns, to tell us what the verbs or objects are, etc. What he does need is a perception of the analogies involved, of the structural differences, and similarities between sentences. It is at this point that language learning becomes the perception of a pattern or configurations of patterns. Without necessarily mastering grammatical terminology, the student must be able to see that certain expressions follow definite patterns: for example, if in *je vais à l'université*, *à l'université* is replaced by *y*, hence *j'y vais,* then *à l'école* in *je vais à l'école* must also be replaced by *y*, hence *j'y vais*. Likewise, if *je parle à mon ami* can be shifted to the past tense *j'ai parlé à mon ami,* then *je trouve mon ami* can be shifted to *j'ai trouvé mon ami,* etc. The ability to see such relations is partly a function of "scholastic aptitude" or "Intelligence" as measured in most of the conventional I.Q. or scholastic or verbal aptitude examinations. It seems thus inevitable that we should find some correlation between a student's general intelligence and his ability to control the pattern mechanism of a foreign language. Experimentation and research on language aptitude have shown that the ability to recognize the function of words and to infer the rules and patterns inductively are essential for success in language learning, apparently regardless of what particular teaching method is used. While transformation and substitution exercises operate on a stimulus-response basis, the very fact that we arrange them according to patterns indicates an appeal to the student's ability to perceive these patterns. Thus the pattern practice approach is essentially a middle of the road approach. It is an attempt to establish responses while at the same time showing the student the pattern involved in the responses. It combines a purely mechanical stimulus response approach which utilizes the student's intelligence, and an attempt to teach the student a method by which he can transfer linguistic patterns to new situations through a transformation or substitution procedure.

The curious fact about second language learning is that two of its major psychological aspects, namely pattern perception and habit formation, are in potential conflict with each other; for the temptation is very strong to substitute the perception of the existence of a pattern for its actual acquisition as a part of one's habitual, automatic performance. The student who has either learned or perceived that "expressions like *à l'école* or *à l'université* can be replaced by *y*" is often unwilling to go through exercises in which this realization is to be transformed into an automatic habit. As a matter of fact he may be so happy with his discovery of this relationship that he is unwilling to have the actual operation of using *y* in response to *à l'école, à l'université,* or *à l'église* become part of his subconscious rather than conscious behavior and reaction. The failure of some highly intelligent students to become really proficient in a foreign language is undoubtedly often due to their unwillingness to perform automatically and their insistence on complete, intellectual realization of all the details involved in their various performances.

An analogy may perhaps elucidate the point made above: if we teach someone to drive a car using a manual shift we have to point out to him how to shift gears. The pattern involved in the process has to become clear. We show how to depress the clutch pedal while releasing the accelerator and shifting the gear while retaining the control of the car, which involves using both feet and both hands. This explanation of the pattern is necessary but no one will ever assume that the explanation alone will teach the student how to shift gears. The only thing that will teach it is the student's performing the act of shifting, correctly and repeatedly. No driving teacher will take it for granted that his student has mastered the skill because he can describe the pattern involved in the act, or even because he has shifted gears a few times correctly. Again, the actual realization of the pattern must be put out of the realm of consciousness if the student is ever to learn to drive a car. We cannot indeed conceive of any driver who every time he shifts gears says to himself in his mind "I am now putting the left foot on the clutch, I am depressing it, while the other foot is off the accelerator, and my right hand is shifting the gear while the other is steering the car." Some driving this would be! Perhaps the driver may pass his test though it is very doubtful. In the same way the student who says, upon answering a question, "The noun stays at the head of the sentence, then comes the pronoun, then the verb," may perhaps pass his French examination, especially if it is a written examination that allows lots of time for his responses. But he cannot speak French any more than our driver can drive a car in the street.

The potential conflict between the perception and the intellectual awareness of a pattern on the one hand and its automatic performance on the other could conceivably be corrected and perhaps even eliminated if our teaching relied solely on the stimulus $>$ response type of approach. In terms of our comparison, we never explain to our student the complete pattern involved in shifting gears, but we make him put his foot on the clutch pedal, and after he has done this and practiced this, we teach him to depress it. After that we make him associate this act with the handling of the gas pedal, and so on. In other words, instead of presenting a complete pattern, we divide the problem into a small number of **stimulus > response** situations, reward and reinforce each response, build up habitual performance without teaching at first the total pattern as a unit. The same approach can be tried in language instruction. The result could be the practical elimination of the type of intellectual interference that comes from wanting to think about what one is doing when shifting gears.

This approach would drive to an extreme the principle of minimal step-by-step learning. A pattern drill in which we shift singulars to plurals (like, *Le professeur est intelligent > Les professeurs sont intelligents; Mon professeur est intelligent > Mes professeurs sont intelligents*) would have to be broken down into its component parts in such a way that at first only absolutely minimal automatic responses are made. Thus the student being drilled on the singular > plural contrast would first be taught to respond to /ə/ as in *le* with /e/ as in *les*; then he would be asked to respond to /ɔ̃/ (as in *mon*) with /e/ (as in mes), to shift from /a/ to /e/ (to prepare for *la > les*). After this *les, ces, mes, tes, ses*, would be taught as responses to *le, ce, mon, ton, son*. The next drill involves changing *est* to *sont*. Only after all of these responses have been practiced and become automatic would the complete pattern drill be undertaken. The possibility of error is practically eliminated by the absolutely minimal nature of the individual learning step. This kind of teaching which stresses habit formation almost exclusively, relies heavily on the language laboratory.

While it is possible to analyze utterances into small units, it is also true that the components function only because they are in relation to each other, because they form complete patterns. Perception or awareness of the complete pattern underlying any utterance is likely to take place sooner or later and with this awareness the danger inherent in the student's rationalizing and thinking about the pattern will again come into being. We also must keep in mind that the reaction produced in response to the original stimulus must eventually be transferred to other stimuli. In terms of our previous example, plurals are usually not produced in response to singulars. The transfer of the response to a different situation, making it independent of the original stimulus, involves precisely the use of the awareness of the total pattern and those intellectual processes which the method is designed to circumvent in the first place.

There is probably no general cure against the type of interference that comes from clinging to intellectual understanding in favor of automatic responses. It is up to the individual language teacher to recognize this problem and deal with it according to circumstances.

This transition from the realization of the existence of a pattern to its automatization can be accomplished in several ways: in some cases the language teacher may simply have to convince the student that he needs further drill and participation in class and laboratory exercises even though he has "understood what it is all about." In other cases, the teacher will run into individuals who are perfectly capable of perceiving a pattern but who practically refuse to take part in the drill exercises and automatization of the pattern unless they receive some sort of intellectual "explanation." In many cases in which this kind of explanation is asked for, the experienced teacher will give a quick explanation which, as such, does not contribute significantly to the performance of the student, but relieves the student's anxiety so that he can then proceed with the real business at hand, namely the drill of the grammatical pattern. To give an example, a grammar book may contain a series of sample sentences—or the teacher may give them on the board— such as (1) *Vous allez à l'école,—Oui j'y vais;* (2) *Vous pensez à la leçon,—Oui, j'y pense;* (3) *Vous arrivez à la gare,—Oui j'y arrive.* These sample sentences may then be contrasted with (1) *Vous parlez à Robert. Oui, je lui parle. Vous obéissez à Charles. Oui, je lui obéis.* The student who has perceived the fact that "*à*"-something is replaced by the pronoun *y* has understood the grammatical point these sentences are meant to illustrate. Whether he can state this rule, whether he can identify the words involved as nouns or pronominal adverbs does not make much difference. Still the teacher (and the textbook) must be prepared for the student who will ask "Just why is the word *y* used in all of these sentences as replacement of those expressions?" A statement like "the pronominal adverb *y* is used to replace a prepositional phrase beginning with *à, sur, en, dans*, provided the noun it replaces is not a person," contributes little to the student's awareness of the pattern, but it may relieve his "intellectual anxiety" and allow him to proceed in his actual learning processes.

Another trick to get the student to perform automatically is to divert his attention from the complexity of the pattern itself. This approach should be stressed especially in connection with patterns which are so complicated that intellectual assembly and synthesis is necessarily doomed to failure. A sequence like *Je ne le lui ai pas donné hier* assembled by intellectual processes cannot be made automatic if the student insists that he has to "think out what he is doing first." Usually a student can be made to produce such a sentence automatically by having his attention diverted from the complicated structure to another point of the utterance; for example, we ask the student to go through a substitution exercise in which the replacement of *hier* by *aujourd'hui, ce matin,* or *trop tard,* is apparently the main focus of the drill.

Perhaps the best way of overcoming the student's concern with the pattern itself rather than with its automatic use is to give him the opportunity to use the pattern in context—to make him talk about something that interests him more than the pattern itself. Of course this approach should not be confused with making the student talk before he has learned the pattern at all. This will only force him into making mistakes. But to combine pattern drill with a meaningful context which in fact disguises the drill is a quite different matter. For example, we can tell a story about a man *"qui n'a pas d'amis," "qui n'a pas d'argent," "qui essaie de trouver une place,"* and *"qui n'a pas de succès."* We can then ask questions about this man: *Est-ce qu'il a du succès? Est-ce qu'il a des amis? Est-ce qu'il a de l'argent?* All these questions amount to a pattern drill in which the student answers with *il n'en a pas,* but the meaningful context which diverts the student's attention from the pattern will contribute to the automatization process.

As far as interference (or negative transfer) is concerned, there are several ways to minimize its possible effects. As we shall stress again later, the complete avoidance of English, as in the direct method, is by itself no guarantee that interference will not take place. On the other hand, it seems only logical to assume that the continuous juxtaposition of English and French in the classroom will encourage interference. As we shall point out in the next chapter, there seem to be certain reasons for a justifiable use of English. Nevertheless as much as possible and in as long stretches as possible the French class should be conducted in French. It is extremely important to create a situation and environment which the student associates with French, in which he expects French stimuli and responses, in which, to use the psychological technical term, his entire mental "set" is keyed to the French language.

Another way of attacking interference—a rather startling one, but one that has been proved feasible by some experimentation—is to eliminate meaning, and with it the main reason for interference, almost totally from the initial phases of language instruction. It is entirely possible to teach the major patterns of a foreign language without letting the student know what he is saying. For instance, the class could learn to shift statements like *ils trouvent les livres, ils cherchent les livres, ils choisissent les livres,* to *nous cherchons les livres,* et cetera. Or the students could be taught to respond automatically to *Est-ce que vous cherchez le livre?* with *nous cherchons le livre*, and on that model they could respond to *Est-ce que vous choisissez?* with *Nous choisissons*, even if they did not know what they were saying. As far as they are concerned, they would simply hear a stimulus *est-ce que vous . . . -ez?* to which they are trained to respond automatically with *nous . . . -ons*. By this procedure the grammar patterns would be acquired. The next step might be to tell the students what the meaning of these grammatical patterns is (for the above example: "I am asking a question and you are answering it"). Only *after* the student has gained complete and automatic control over the grammatical patterns would he be acquainted with the precise meaning of what he has learned. This means that the temptation to construct French in terms of English (*"nous cherchons pour le livre"*) could practically be eliminated. At least, by the time it is introduced the student would be well fortified against it.

The teaching of grammar patterns independently and before the introduction of the meaning of words is one of the new possibilities and new frontiers of language teaching which have been opened up as a result of linguistic analysis, especially because of the increasing availability of language laboratories. Detailed programs of French courses putting this kind of teaching into operation still have to be worked out; just how much interference could reappear in such courses, after meaning has been introduced, remains to be seen.

Perhaps the most promising way of combatting interference or negative transfer is, of course, to start the student's learning process at an age when negative transfer or interference seems slight, or at least readily overcome—depending on the individual, perhaps before age ten or eleven. At the same time, those who advocate the "early start" should be aware of the fact that their case seems to rest primarily on **avoidance of interference** or negative transfer, rather than on maximization of positive transfer. In other words, we have no definite proof at this point that the child's resistance to interference or negative transfer may not be—in part at least—the result of a less developed ability to transfer under any circumstance, positive or negative. If this is so, early language training may appear uneconomical in some respects and would in any case have to be fairly intensive.

It would seem that perhaps the best way of avoiding negative transfer in any learning situation might be to concentrate on stimulus > response learning—in other words, intensive practice—in the areas in which interference is likely to occur. Transfer can do the job in areas where it is likely to be positive, but we must rely on practice where it is likely to be negative. In terms of our initial example, phrases like *il est stupide, il est bon, il est méchant* do not need to be drilled; *il a froid, il a chaud, il a peur,* et cetera, must be the object of extensive practice.

CHAPTER IV

Linguistic and Nonlinguistic Teaching Procedures

Having in mind the general specifications of a "linguistic" method as discussed in the previous chapters, we can now take a look in more detail at the way in which a linguistic methodology affects the language classroom. In connection with this we shall examine some of the facets of teaching procedures which seem of greatest interest to every language teacher: the use of English in the classroom, the types of exercises to be used in language drill, the organization of the individual lessons and the use of visual aids.

(A) THE USE OF ENGLISH IN THE FRENCH CLASS

Some of what can be stated here has been implied in our discussion of the direct method: since in a linguistic approach we want to concentrate as much as possible on specific drills dealing with specific problems, we can use English for the purpose of economy. A brief explanation or an "attention-pointer" given in English may save time. At certain stages of the course it may be possible to give explanations in French, and such explanations will afford a certain amount of language practice to the student. But he will be listening to a great variety of structures, some of which may still be unfamiliar to him. He may not, as a result, understand the teacher. He may become bewildered and his mind may wander from the particular problem which was under discussion in the first place. The practice he is getting in listening to the teacher is not organized around a particular problem; it is not part of the overall learning scheme of the course. Thus a brief explanation in English may save time for more concentrated learning and avoid disorganization and confusion.

Translation or explanation in English may also be the most economical way of supplying the meaning of structure, and especially of vocabulary items. Here again the arbitrary avoidance of English makes it not only difficult to arrange the material according to linguistic patterns, it may, especially in the case of fairly obvious vocabulary items, lead to rather involved and unnecessarily lengthy explanation. It is perfectly true that building stones of different languages should not be equated. But the danger involved in making these equations is especially great with words like for, about, when, will, shall, by, and so on. Those little words which form or determine the overall shape of the construction have been compared by some linguists to the mortar of the construction rather than to the stones themselves. Obviously no English explanation or translation should even be attempted for these words which have the primary purpose of denoting grammatical relationships and which we shall call the construction or **function words** of the language. But with words which denote obvious concepts and above all easily identifiable physical objects, the danger involved in giving French-English equations may not be very great. Even if the equation is not given by the teacher, it may be supplied by the student anyway. Thus if a student meets a sentence like *je voudrais que vous envoyiez ce paquet tout de suite* and he is in doubt as to the meaning of *paquet*, it is probably better to explain that *paquet* means package rather than to attempt to define the word in French—a procedure which will take the student's mind off the construction which he is studying and which is the real problem of the above sentence.

Other reasons for the possible use of English in a French class go beyond the realm of economy, but have an independent linguistic and pedagogical justification of their own. Difficulties usually revolve around contrast between English and French. The use of English makes it possible to focus attention on those contrasts and drive them home to the learner. The most obvious example of the principle involved here comes from the realm of phonology and will be discussed with more examples and in greater detail at a later point in this book: a speaker of English will have difficulty in the pronunciation of certain French sounds because he will tend to substitute English sounds for those of French. Thus for the vowel of French *gai* he might substitute the vowel of English gay. One way of combatting this mistake is to contrast the English and French sounds for the student, make him conscious of the difference, teach him to identify the French and the English sounds.

This principle of overtly contrasting English and French can also be applied in the realm of constructions. Thus a drill in which the student substitutes different nouns in a construction like *Je veux que vous appreniez la leçon* can be preceded by an overt comparison of that construction with the English I want you to study the lesson. Moreover, the contrast between English and French itself can be made part of the pattern drill in which the teacher asks the student to translate sentences like, I want you to study the lesson, I want you to study the book, I want you to study the rule, and the student in fact goes through a pattern drill exercise which impresses a structural difference between English and French upon his memory.

From the linguistic point of view, it is difficult to decide whether this kind of pattern drill which consists of an overt comparison of English and French is more useful than the exercises in which the French structure is drilled in French alone without comparison with English. The answer depends no doubt on psychological factors involving the student, his age, aptitude, and so on. One thing can, however, be pointed out from the linguistic point of view, namely that this kind of drill should be performed orally. There are at least two reasons for this: using the native language as an oral stimulus minimizes the danger of the student's using the English sentence as a basis for word-for-word translation. Seeing English sentences written out gives the student time to "figure out" correspondences between English and French building stones, the activity which we have characterized as the archenemy of successful language learning. Once the overt comparison between English and French has been made, English should not be used as a basis for word-by-word translation, but only as a stimulus to provoke a French construction already known *in toto* by the student. The response triggered by the English I want you to study that idea must be an automatic *Je veux que vous étudiiez cette idée*, and not a slow *Je veux . . . Je vous veux . . .* et cetera. It is only through oral practice that we can make sure of that particular nature of the response.

The other reason for insisting on limiting oneself to the use of *oral* English as the stimulus for French is the simple fact that in some cases only oral English allows us to make an accurate comparison. Thus the difference between *un professeur de français* and *un professeur français* is expressed in English by a difference in stress: *un professeur de français* is a French‾| teacher (heavier stress on French), while *un professeur français* is a French |‾teacher (heavier stress on teacher). In English different parts of the sentence may be stressed with a resultant difference in meaning. John ⏋ wants that book (stress on John) means that John and not someone else, wants the book; John wants ⎡ that ⏋ book (stress on that) means that John wants that particular book, and not a different one; John wants that ⎡ book (stress on book) means that John wants the book and no other object. In French, such differences of meaning are conveyed by differences in structure rather than by stress. Thus the students whom we want to put through a pattern exercise drilling the French emphasis construction (for example, *C'est moi qui ai fait cela*) should be made aware that the French construction corresponds to the English use of emphatic stress and their French responses may then be triggered by English sentences like I⏋ did it, I⏋ saw it, I⏋ read it (all with heaviest stress on I).

The positive advantage of the deliberate, but limited, use of English lies thus in showing and drilling the differences between English and French. This very advantage is lost in many textbooks by the practice of adapting English to French structure to as great an extent as possible. The reason for it is evident: if English is used as the basis for translation into French, this manipulation of English will lead the student to avoid a translation mistake in the specific sentence on which he happens to be operating. At the same time it is obvious that the student who has said *C'est lui qui a fait cela* only in response to the structure It is he who has done that may well contrive to express He ⏋ did it (heavy stress on he) with Il ⎡ a fait cela (stressing the unstressed subject pronoun!), an erroneous and meaningless procedure in French. Since he uses the French emphasis construction only in response to something that he would most likely never say in English, he will probably never use it in French either. The same may apply to the student whose response *On parle anglais* has always been triggered by One speaks English and never by They speak English or English is spoken. I have known students who could translate "One tells me that you are right" quite beautifully into *On me dit que vous avez raison*, but who in free composition or conversation came up with such strange expressions as *Ils me disent* or even worse, "*Je suis dit.*"

Even if there is a choice between two equally good English constructions, one paralleling the French and the other not, I should suggest that the construction clashing with French be made the stimulus of the pattern drill. Of course, the construction of I give the book to Charles prepares the ground very neatly for *Je donne le livre à Charles*, but why should a student be allowed to go wrong whenever he happens to be influenced by I give Charles the book? Certainly the translation of *Il aurait pu aller* by "He would have been able to go" may at times save the teacher and student some trouble since in the English as well as in the French construction to go and *aller* appear in the present infinitive; but the consistent use of "He would have been able" will not teach the student to cope with the problem created by the interference coming from the English He could have gone (= *il aurait pu aller*).

What we have said really adds up to one fundamental point: the English with which French is to be contrasted must be normal English as spoken by the student. It is the student's actual behavior in English that creates the problem. For this reason the accurate and truthful description of the English spoken by our student must be the basis of our comparison and contrast with French since it is the way the student speaks English that creates the problem, not the way he ought to speak. To manipulate the English or to be "prescriptive" about it may only obscure the real point of difficulty and create unnecessary confusion. Many French grammars go into long explanations about the French equivalents of I should give (*Je donnerais* vs. *Je devrais donner*) trying to solve a problem created by the assumption that the student uses or at least ought to use "should" as the first person corresponding to He would. The fact is that most students never use should as a conditional anyway, and understand *Je donnerais* perfectly well as I would give, (I'd give) and *Je devrais donner* as I ought to (or should) give.

Of course the main abuse of English in the French class lies simply in using it too much. After all French can only be practiced by speaking French. English explanations, no matter how accurate or elegant, will never take the place of practice. Even the suggested use of English in pattern drills should be put into practice judiciously and sparingly, because **the use of English as stimulus for French does not correspond to a normal speaking situation**, nor does it give the student the same practice in auditory comprehension that is afforded by a French stimulus. We defend English in the French class primarily as an economy measure to free class time for more practice in speaking French patterns. The excessive use of English and the constant switching from English to French defeats its own purpose and cannot be justified by any possible pedagogical, linguistic, or psychological argument.

(B) TYPES OF DRILLS AND EXERCISES

The mainstay of the linguistically oriented drill is **stimulus in French**. We have already characterized substitution and transformation as the main features of linguistic drill. We shall presently take a closer look at them and contrast them with other types of teaching devices.

In a sentence like: *Je voudrais que vous répondiez à ces lettres*, we are dealing with a rather complex French structure which offers several difficulties to a speaker of English: It clashes with the English pattern expressed by I'd like you to answer these letters, or I want you to answer these letters. The French construction requires the use of a subjunctive in the subordinate clause; answer requires a direct object; *répondre* requires the preposition *à*. Thus, whether or not we point out these difficulties to the student, the construction must be made the object of a special drill; perhaps the initial step in such a drill may be the repetition of the sentence itself. But a single sentence by itself does not teach a pattern. We shall therefore ask our student to substitute *mes questions, mes enquêtes* in the original sentence. The substitution of these items will not cause any great difficulty to the student. They change nothing in the structure as such; they do not require the formulation of new subjunctives, nor changes in person or tense. Thus substitution is basically a way of making the student repeat the pattern, making it a matter of habit. After these sentences have been drilled this way, we may ask the student to substitute *mes ordres, mes amis, obéissiez, pensiez, parliez,* then *j'exige, j'insiste,* and so on, so that the final response of the student may be a sentence like: *J'insiste que vous parliez à mes amis.*

In the last response the overall pattern which has remained constant during the exercise is the same as it was in the first line; but except for the small function words involved (*je . . . que . . . à . . .*) the vocabulary items have changed. In spite of this there is still a certain identity of meaning that was also kept constant during the exercise, namely, I, would like, want, expect, you to do something. This part of the meaning of the sentence is not identical with the sum of the **lexical meanings** of the vocabulary items involved, but it is the **meaning of the structure,** of the pattern itself. A structure or pattern may therefore be identified as the **common element of different sentences or phrases which have the same structural meaning.** Strictly speaking, a single French sentence can thus be only an example of a pattern: by itself it can neither be a pattern nor can it teach one. The **pattern** is the grammatical relationship itself and the structural meaning expressed by the sentence.

The pattern of:

Je	voudrais	que	vous	répondiez	à ces	lettres

may thus be thought of as a structure or frame in which only the function words and endings indicating grammatical relationships remain constant. The lexical items can be exchanged with others. The purpose of the substitution exercise is then the teaching of the pattern itself and the teaching of its structural meaning.

It will be seen quite clearly that the **transformation** type of exercise has the same purpose. The substitution exercise exchanges lexical items and keeps the structural meaning, or the pattern, constant. In the transformation exercise we take different examples of the same pattern and by repetition of the same operation transform them into a new pattern or construction.

Le professeur étudie le français.	> *Le professeur étudie-t-il le français?*
Le médecin cherche le livre.	> *Le médecin cherche-t-il le livre?*
Le garçon trouve le crayon.	> *Le garçon trouve-t-il le crayon?*

All the sentences in each of the two columns above follow identical patterns and the element differentiating them is represented by the addition of *-t-il* (plus a change in intonation).

That all other types of pattern practice are basically related to substitution or transformation will be seen quite easily:

Expansion involves enlarging a frame by adding a new element. It is therefore a type of transformation. The sentence: *J'ai vu le professeur,* may be expanded by the addition of the element *souvent:*

J'ai souvent vu le professeur.

And likewise:

J'ai recontré le professeur.

J'ai souvent rencontré le professeur.

Replacement (of nouns by pronouns, for instance) involves a regular change of one frame to another, and it is again a type of **transformation.**

J'ai vu le livre.	> *Je l'ai vu.*
J'ai regardé le film.	> *Je l'airegardé.*
J'ai cherché le crayon.	> *Je l'ai cherché.*

Transformation in echelon is a special type of transformation exercise which starts by changing one element of the frame and then introduces gradually other simultaneous transformation operations.

(a) *Cherchez-vous le livre?*	> *Je cherche le livre.*
Trouvez-vous le livre?	> *Je trouve le livre.*

(b) *Cherchez-vous le livre?* > *Je le cherche.*
    Trouvez-vous le livre? > *Je le trouve.*

(c) *Cherchez-vous le livre?* > *Je ne le cherche pas.*
    Trouvez-vous le livre? > *Je ne le trouve pas.*

Transformation and substitution are often combined in the same exercise. For example, a substitution of a different subject will necessitate a transformation of the verb form:

Je cherche *le livre.* > **Nous cherchons** *le livre.*
Je trouve *le livre.* > **Nous trouvons** *le livre.*
Je regarde *le tableau.* > **Nous regardons** *le tableau.*

Restatement exercises are basically rather complicated forms of transformations involving several simultaneous operations:

Dites à Charles qu'il étudie le français. > *Vous étudiez le français.*
Dites à Robert qu'il regarde le livre. > *Vous regardez le livre.*
Dites à Jean qu'il cherche le crayon. > *Vous cherchez le crayon.*

In all types of pattern practice exercises, especially in those based on transformation, it is advisable to keep in mind that simple transformation involving only a minimal operation should be drilled first before the student is asked to go through complex operations. In many transformation or expansion exercises, the completely automatic response will also have to be replaced eventually by a response involving a choice on the part of the student. This involves all the cases in which French makes exceptions to its own patterns. In such cases the pattern and the exception must be drilled thoroughly and independently before the exercise involving choice between two patterns is presented to the student. The response, let us say, in:

J'obéis à Robert. > *Je lui obéis.*
Je parle à Robert. > *Je lui parle.*

and in:

Je pense à Robert. > *Je pense à lui.*
Je songe à Charles. > *Je songe à lui.*

must be firmly established before an exercise in which several patterns are mixed is presented to the student:

J'obéis à Robert. > *Je lui obéis.*
Je pense à Robert. > *Je pense à lui.*
Je parle à Jean. > *Je lui parle.*

There is no doubt that some students at least may find the types of pattern practice just described somewhat tedious or boring. No doubt it can be for some. The points to be made here are simply that (1) repetition is not supposed to replace the analytic understanding of the construction, but (2) it alone can assure **automatic response**, and (3) it leads to successful manipulation of language skills on the part of many students who would be unable to construct a sentence by a purely analytical approach.

Of course pattern practice is not meant to be the only type of exercise or practice to be used in a language class. Pattern practice is a means to an end. The end to be achieved is the ability to use the language freely, as in exercises of the more traditional type in which students ask or are asked questions about a story or are engaged in conversation on a specific topic. The point is that the question-and-answer type of exercise or the free conversation are usually a test of whether or not the patterns have been learned, rather than a way of practicing the patterns. The pattern practice may be compared to the exercise and drills that a football or basketball player must undergo in order to be ready and fit for a game. Certainly the game as such is the interesting part and the culmination of the effort. To do nothing but pattern practice would be very much like putting someone through football practice without ever giving him a chance to play. No coach would do this—but neither would he put anyone on the team who has not gone through a rigorous training in all the little detailed operations which make up the skill of the football players.

What we have said about questions and answers and conversation applies also to many of the other traditional kinds of exercises. Most of them are really tests of whether or not learning has taken place rather than teaching procedures themselves. It is of course true that a test given over and over again can become a teaching instrument; but teaching through testing, which may be teaching through letting the student make mistakes, is not a very efficient procedure.

Perhaps the old fashioned type of translation exercise in which examples of different patterns are scrambled up in, let us say, ten or twenty sentences to be put into French is the best example of what a teaching device should not be like.

Suppose we give the student a lesson about the present subjunctive, explain its formation, then tell him that the present subjunctive is used after verbs of emotion, verbs of thinking in the negative, verbs expressing doubt, verbs expressing volition and impersonal expressions (except those denoting certainty), and so on. Each one of these rules may be illustrated by one or more examples. Then we ask the student to translate sentences like:

> Do you think that he is right?
> We doubt that he will arrive tomorrow.
> Let's not be afraid.
> It is not necessary for you to read these papers.
> I expect all of you to do your duty.

The above sentences translated into French are examples of many different patterns. Practically the only feature they have in common is that in each of these patterns, one of the building stones used is an ending which we can identify as the present subjunctive. But this is not enough to establish any identity or even great similarity between the patterns themselves. Actually, this exercise does not teach the pattern. It tests whether or not the student has already been able to recognize the underlying patterns from the rules and the few examples alone. Every language teacher knows that only the most intelligent and analytical students are able to do this, and even those students are not able to give anything like an automatic or spontaneous response.

Another favorite type of traditional exercise consists of French sentences, parts of which are either left blank or replaced by English expressions. A variation of this type of exercise is the French sentence for which the verb is supplied in the infinitive and is to be put into the the real form required by the sentence:

> *Je veux que vous* (leave:) *tout de suite.*
> *Je veux que vous* (*partir:*   ) *tout de suite.*

As far as type A is concerned, we must first of all protest against the hybrid English/French sentence which gives the impression that English building stones or their "equivalents" can be made to fit into a French construction. As far as type B is concerned, this may make some sense as a test in which we want to pin the student down on one single point (probably for the sake of objective scoring). As teaching devices these types of exercises have only a limited value precisely because they do not force the student to produce complete patterns. After all, it is the entire pattern that has to be learned and that must become one of the student's speech habits. The student should not be made to chisel, so to speak, on only one building stone in order to make it fit into the construction.

(C) LESSON ORGANIZATION

What we have seen so far concerning types of drills and linguistic teaching methodology has of course an immediate bearing on the overall organization of the lesson and of the textbook. Any lesson organization which makes it impossible to have specific drills with a single emphasis on the new construction or vocabulary problem to be learned will be counter to linguistic principle.

The most obvious offender against linguistic principle is the lesson which consists of a set of grammatical rules (more or less extensively illustrated by examples), a series of vocabulary items, and exercises in which the student is expected to apply the grammatical rules and the vocabulary items, thus manufacturing French—usually his own brand— according to a set of recipes.

The type of organization which deals with a single point of grammar, like the negative or the subjunctive is not necessarily a saving device. As we have pointed out before, such classifications as the subjunctive or the negative may be, and often are, used to assemble a multitude of quite divergent structures of varying difficulty under a single heading. Moreover, the teacher who organizes his material according to such large grammatical categories will often fall victim to the temptation of covering the category in one lesson. This desire to be "complete" is understandable enough on the part of the teacher who knows the material and organizes it in his own way. But the organization which seems most logical and appropriate to the person who already knows the language is not necessarily the one that is pedagogically, most suitable. We must learn to resist the temptation to give the rule, the exception to the rule, and the exception to the exception in one and the same lesson. The student who is trying to grasp the rather difficult construction of the partitive need not be told in the same lesson and within the same breath that the partitive after *beaucoup*, *assez*, et cetera, is expressed by *de*, that after *plupart* it is *des*, and that after *ni . . . ni . . .* there is no partitive at all. Keeping in mind that learning a language means establishing patterns of behavior, it seems highly inappropriate to introduce exceptions to and complications of a pattern before the basic pattern itself has been firmly established by repetition and practice.

Another tempting but often inadvisable way of organizing the lesson is to take a semantic rather than a grammatical category as the basic unit of organization. One possibility is to organize around basic units of experience. This organization, usually tied in with the direct method, results in lessons built around experiences like *le déjeuner, au théâtre, à la gare,* et cetera. Like the direct method itself, this approach is not *necessarily* in conflict with linguistic teaching; but it does take a great deal of careful planning to make the two compatible. Evaluating a lesson like *le déjeuner* or *Noël en France,* the linguistically oriented pedagogue will not be primarily concerned with the questions, "How lively and interesting is the story?" or "How many useful expressions does it contain?" His main concern will be "Does it contain new structures which are of particular difficulty for speakers of English?" "Are such structures singled out for specific and systematic drill?", and "Does it contain vocabulary problems that are *not* dealt with in specific exercises?"

Another possible semantic category for organizing the lesson is the "concept approach." The latter utilizes such categories as "the ways of expressing the future," "the immediate past," "the idea of obligation," et cetera. Much can be said for this type of organization, especially on the more advanced level of language teaching; it does present the material organized according to the viewpoint of the speaker wanting to use the particular language. It presents the grammatical and stylistic choices which the speaker must know in order to be able to communicate his thoughts. At the same time, it seems almost impossible to use this concept approach as the main guide for the organization of an elementary language class, for too many completely different and linguistically unrelated structures would have to be thrown together into the same lesson if the approach were to be followed through: a lesson dealing with the expression of the "immediate past" would have to contain the *venir de* + infinitive construction as well as that of *tout à l'heure.* A lesson dealing with the ways of expressing the immediate future would have to include a number of constructions such as *aller* + infinitive, *s'en aller* + infinitive, *être pour* + infinitive, *être sur le point de* + infinitive, and the adverbs *bientôt, immédiatement, avant peu, tout à l'heure.*

Perhaps the most important point to keep in mind in the organization of linguistically oriented teaching materials is that for any approach which relies primarily on habit formation, the unit of instruction is not the lesson or chapter but the individual exercise: the drill dealing with a specific structure which adds a new building stone to the student's repertory. This does not mean that such an approach to language teaching is atomistic and that it does not see the overall problem. On the contrary, it looks at the student's acquisition of the language as a chain in which the individual exercises are the links that must be carefully connected with each other. If an exercise includes several difficulties, or if it builds on problems not previously taught, this chain will be broken and the student's knowledge will become fragmentary. But language study viewed as the formation of linguistic habit is a *continuum*, a progression from one link of the chain to the next, a progression which preferably should be allowed only after each link is solidly fashioned and anchored to its predecessor.

If we organize our teaching materials as single-emphasis drills, each one designed to establish a particular speech pattern, each drill, in a sense, becomes a lesson in itself and the lesson as an overall unit of organization becomes a quite arbitrary unit. Linguistically oriented materials are thus apt to form a continuum of drills and exercises. Accompanying this continuum there should be, of course, exercises for review, examples of connected speech and stories (perhaps the "unit of experience" type) which provide a meaningful context for the learning of vocabulary and for the practice of the speech patterns acquired by the student. The typical lesson or unit might thus consist of, let us say, ten individual drills, followed by a story in which the ten patterns, presented in those drills, are used in context; following this, there might be a series of questions about the story, which would give the student the opportunity to use the ten patterns in his answers. A variation of this organization might be to introduce the new patterns in the context of the story, then have the drills dealing with the new patterns, and the questions and answers calling for the contextual use of the patterns.

(D) VISUAL AIDS

There are various types of visual aids and many ways to use them in the language class. We shall comment on some of the most important categories from the linguistic viewpoint, beginning with those which are unrelated to structural linguistic teaching.

The most obvious way of using pictures is, of course, to employ them for the teaching of vocabulary items: the teacher may hold up a picture of a horse to the class, point to it, and utter the word *cheval*. He may then ask a question like *Qu'est-ce que c'est?* in the hope of eliciting the response *C'est un cheval* from the class. Useful as this kind of pictorial aid may be it has no immediate relation to the teaching of language structures.

Another possible use of the picture is the description of a scene or action. A picture is presented to the student: the words for all the persons or objects in the picture and the actions taking place are then described. Then the student is asked questions about what is going on. This kind of pictorial aid has several useful applications: if typically French scenes and typically French settings are chosen, a great deal of cultural information can be conveyed. The picture can also be used to good advantage for the contextual presentation of vocabulary items and of structures previously drilled or to be drilled. Since the description of even a very simple picture is apt to call for a variety of forms and patterns, it is an occasion for the use and testing rather than the learning of grammatical patterns.

Quite different use is made of the pictorial aid if it is of the type in which every sentence to be learned by the student is accompanied by one picture. With this kind of pictorial aid two quite distinct possibilities must be differentiated. In the first method the picture is used to convey the exact semantic content of the sentence: the student hears the sentence *Un homme entre dans la salle* and sees the picture of a man entering a room. This kind of visual aid has been elaborated into a rather skillful teaching device, in which stick figures rather than personalized pictures are used. These figures are systematically put through a series of actions which teach the student basic semantic concepts with help of a basic vocabulary. This technique, an elaboration of the direct method, is again nonlinguistic, insofar as it does not take its point of view of organization from the structure of French nor does it in any way consider the particular difficulties of the speaker of English.

The other approach which combines an individual structure with a single picture sees in the picture not a way to convey the exact meaning of that structure, but rather its visual reinforcement. This visual reinforcement is supposed to be doubly effective if the picture is esthetically of high quality (we are at the opposite pole from the stick figures). The actual connection between the meaning of the sentence to be learned and the picture may be quite loose. Let us say, a picture of people skiing is accompanied by a sentence like *Les Français aiment aussi les sports d'hiver*. The value of this kind of use of pictures, aside from the obvious possibilities in the representation of a French cultural environment, lies in the supposed reinforcement of the structure to be learned. Whether such a reinforcement actually takes place (could it be that the visual impact rather diverts the student's attention from the language structure?) remains to be confirmed by experiments. Again, there is no obvious connection between the linguistic structural teaching approach and the pictorial aid.

A more linguistic use of the pictorial aid is made when it serves to teach a vocabulary item or construction which is difficult to learn because of the interference coming from the English speech habits. Such pictorial aids may for instance be used to reinforce the teaching of the "false cognates" or "*faux amis.*" These vocabulary items resemble English words in form but have quite different meanings: a picture of a man sitting in passive enjoyment of a concert may illustrate *assister au concert*; or that of a man entering a bookstore may drive home the real meaning of *librairie*. We may also use pictures to illustrate the meaning of *il a chaud* vs. *il fait chaud*, or *le café est chaud*.

Pictorial aids may also be brought into play in order to teach concepts and contrasts which are lacking in the native language. This includes, for example, the familiar type of line graphs which illustrate the meaning of different tenses such as the imperfect vs. the *passé composé*.

A very direct application of the structural linguistic approach to the use of visual aids is the structural diagraming of sentence patterns. Various examples of the same pattern are presented to the student in such a way that the elements which fulfill identical functions in the pattern are lined up vertically and are put into the same slot in the structural frame:

Nous	connaiss	ons	ce	garçon
Nous	appren	ons	notre	leçon
Nous	trouv	ons	votre	livre

The same method can also be used in the visual presentation of substitution exercises:

	Je	veux	que	vous	sortiez	tout de suite.
1.	—	demande	—	—	—	—
2.	—	exige	—	—	—	—
3.	—	—	—	—	partiez	—
	—	—	—	—	—	immédiatement.

This type of presentation is an important aid in the teaching of structure. In many ways it is more effective than lengthy grammatical explanation in making the student aware of basic similarities and differences between patterns and in making him conscious of grammatical word classes.

A very direct tie-in between the structural approach and the pictorial aid occurs when the picture chart is used to illustrate a grammatical category. For example, we may compose a chart which shows various actions, all illustrating the verbs conjugated with *être*. Or we may construct a similar chart illustrating the important verbs which take direct objects in French while their normal English counterparts take a prepositional object. Such a chart might show the picture of a man waiting for a bus (*l'homme attend l'autobus*), that of a student looking for a pencil (*l'étudiant cherche le crayon*), a girl listening to the radio (*la jeune fille écoute la radio*).

The composite chart of the type mentioned above is probably the most immediate application of pictorial aids to linguistic teaching, for this type of chart can be used most effectively in the basic drill techniques of substitution, transformation, and expansion. A chart showing several objects or persons can provide the nouns to be substituted in a pattern. The teacher provides the pattern to be drilled—let us say, *Je veux que vous parliez au professeur*, and merely by pointing at different pictures, he elicits the responses *Je veux que vous parliez à la mère, Je veux que vous parliez au soldat, Je veux que vous parliez à la bonne*, et cetera. The same chart may also be used to provide substitution items in a sentence like *C'est un vieux professeur*, to elicit responses like *C'est une vieille bonne, C'est un vieux soldat, C'est une vieille mère*, et cetera.

Even more useful for pattern drills is the chart which is composed of a series of action pictures. The student learns the basic sentence which describes each action taking place on the chart: *Le professeur cherche le livre; l'étudiant attend l'autobus; la mère écoute la radio; l'élève regarde le cahier*. Once each sentence has been learned and associated with the picture, the latter becomes an efficient instrument with which to trigger the student's responses in manipulative pattern drills. For example, the basic sentences may be transformed into different tenses: by pointing at a particular picture and using a key word (for example, *hier*), the teacher may drill his class to respond with a *passé composé: le professeur a cherché le livre; l'étudiant a attendu l'autobus*. The word *demain* may be used to trigger a response in the future; *autrefois* for a response in the imperfect, and so on. The teacher may ask the class or individual students to substitute different subjects in the actions of the chart. He might point at the chart and say *nous* to make the class respond with *nous cherchons le livre*, or *nous écoutons la radio*. The basic sentences may be made negative, transformed into questions, the nouns may be replaced by pronouns, questions may be asked for the subjects or objects of the actions; substitution words (such as an adverb) may be suggested to be inserted into the basic sentences.

The picture chart, if used as described above, becomes then primarily a vehicle for the teaching of structure or grammar. It is definitely not meant as an instrument of the teaching of vocabulary. As a matter of fact, its very advantage is that it permits the use of familiar vocabulary at the time when the student is introduced to a new point of grammar. Once the basic sentences are learned and used over and over again, the student may become almost unaware of the lexical meaning of the sentences and focuses his attention exclusively on the structural transformations: we have gone full circle from the use of the picture to teach vocabulary to its employment in the teaching of structure.

(E) THE LANGUAGE LABORATORY

There is no need to duplicate here the description of laboratory techniques found in several excellent texts which have appeared recently, and which deal primarily with the object of the language laboratory. While the laboratory is, of course, potentially a useful adjunct to any teaching approach, it is particularly useful, sometimes necessary, for the linguistic method. It is in the laboratory that two psychological principles utilized by the linguistic method can find immediate application: (1) that language learning is primarily habit formation and (2) that correct responses are learned better if they are immediately reinforced by reward.

In the classroom only one student can perform at any given time. It is true that by choral responses and answers the teacher may include more than two students in a situation. But the very fact that the student is performing in a group lessens his personal attention, his drives, and his motivation. The reward given for the correct response is directed toward the entire class and is thus less effective than that given to an individual. In any choral response there will be only a few leaders and a large number of the students will be followers. For the latter, the choral response exercise is in fact a repetition rather than a new reaction to a stimulus. But in the laboratory, a large number of students can perform simultaneously. They can be rewarded simultaneously and immediately, for the answer they are supposed to give can be given on the tape. As soon as the student has finished his own response in any pattern drill, as soon as he has answered a question asked on the tape, the correct answer given on the tape can reward and reinforce the correct answer by the student. Even if the student's response has been wrong the opportunity to be corrected immediately and in an impersonal manner is undoubtedly a distinct advantage over the type of correction which occurs hours after the student has made the mistake in his homework, or the type which occurs in front of his fellow students in the classroom. The latter point brings us to perhaps the most essential and obvious contribution of the laboratory: it is the only meaningful way in which the formation of language skills can be made part of the student's "homework." A student sitting in silence in front of a book can hardly learn a language, because he either does not perform, or is likely to perform wrongly. He may perhaps develop some understanding of the patterns he is trying to analyze, though it is rather doubtful that he will develop this understanding by himself at home if he did not achieve it in the classroom under the guidance of the teacher. The main contribution homework can make is in the automatization of the responses, in fixing the correct answers in the student's mind. Where else but in the language laboratory (or in the presence of a private tutor) could this essential and (on the elementary level) only real function of homework be guaranteed? It seems thus that the laboratory functions best and can make its major contribution when it can be used in addition to or in conjunction with, rather than in lieu of, classroom instruction, and when it can assure flexibility in the amount of time needed by individual students to achieve mastery of learning tasks according to their individual needs and abilities.

The laboratory is no doubt the best place in which to locate the stimulus-response type of learning, the manipulation of patterns in transformation and substitution drill. The classroom is the place for explanation and above all for the use of the speech pattern in a situational context. In terms of a comparison we made earlier between language learning and football training, the laboratory is the practice field, the gymnasium, in which detailed operations involved in the game are drilled, and the classroom is the football field in which the actual game takes place. This does not mean that at times it may not be necessary to make their functions overlap. Obviously we may sometimes practice patterns in the classroom, and in turn, may sometimes prepare for the laboratory a little story followed by questions concerning it. There are many ways of enlivening laboratory work, but even then, the instructor planning the course should always keep in mind the principle that the laboratory and classroom are utilized best if there is division, rather than a duplication, of work between the two.

The more we emphasize habit formation in our teaching, the more the laboratory moves from the position of an adjunct to the language course to that of its very center in which all essential learning takes place. The concept of habit formation by the immediate reward of correct responses has recently been combined with the idea of minimal step learning in the "Teaching Machine" approach in "programmed" French courses. In any kind of programming the material to be learned is broken down into a number of learning steps or frames. At the end of each step an answer—hopefully the correct one—is elicited from the student. Only the correct answer is confirmed or otherwise rewarded. In programmed learning, the laboratory becomes indeed the private tutor of the individual student: responding to the stimuli provided by the machine, the student checks the accuracy of his answers against those provided by the machine. Ideally, the laboratory should then also furnish some sort of mechanical signal which confirms and further reinforces the correct response. It should also provide some sort of check which would allow the student to proceed to a new learning step only after the previous step has been thoroughly mastered. The possibility of incorporating these last two requirements to audio-lingual learning in the laboratory has been experimented with in various programmed courses. While at the writing of this text none of the programmed French courses have had any large scale application, it seems that programming, especially audio-lingual programming, will become an important part of foreign language teaching. Some of the details and assumptions concerning programmed learning, such as the underlying theory of learning, role of student motivation, and size of the individual learning step, are still, and will undoubtedly remain, subject to dispute. But there is no doubt that programming can make a very significant contribution in at least one area that has been of concern to teachers. The individual student can be allowed to proceed at his own speed and the language laboratory as a teaching machine can be used to eliminate or at least alleviate the classroom situation which forces the slow and fast learner into the same learning pace.

PART TWO

CHAPTER V

General Phonetics and Phonemics

(A) PHONETICS

The raw material of language consists of sounds. The science which is concerned with the study of speech sounds is **phonetics**. Phonetics can approach the study of speech sounds from two very different points of view: it can study the properties of the sounds themselves, that is, the exact nature of the sound waves as they progress through the air; or it can study the way in which the sounds are produced by the human speech organs. That branch of phonetics which studies the sounds themselves is called **acoustic phonetics**, and the study of the sound production is called **articulatory phonetics**. Acoustic phonetics has made important strides during the past years, as the result of the discovery and perfection of machines which allow us to analyze the speech sounds in great detail. But from the viewpoint of the language teacher, articulatory phonetics will continue to be the more important branch of phonetics.

There are several good textbooks in existence, all dealing in great detail with the science of articulatory phonetics. In this chapter we shall, therefore, summarize and review the most important concepts of phonetics which are useful to the teacher of French, rather than try to give a detailed account of the discipline. Phoneticians have for some time been concerned with the creation of a phonetic alphabet. They have worked out and are still perfecting an **international phonetic alphabet**. Ideally, such an alphabet would have one symbol and one symbol only to identify without ambiguity any speech sound possible in any of the languages existing today. In presenting the resumé of phonetics we shall emphasize only those sounds and symbols which are of importance for the French teacher. We shall follow the customary procedure of presenting phonetic transcriptions within square brackets: [ ].

Speech sounds are traditionally classified as vowels and consonants. In the production of vowels the air stream passes through the larynx over the vocal cords, and their vibration creates sounds which are modified in the oral cavity by the other speech organs. At no time during the production of the sound is the air stream interrupted or impeded. In the production of the consonants, however, the airstream meets a definite obstacle while passing through the speech organs, which impedes or momentarily stops the sound.

Turning our attention first to the classification of consonants, we find that there are three possible criteria according to which they can be described. The first classification considers the already mentioned activity of the vocal cords. The actual mechanism which correlates the vibration of the vocal cords and the production of a consonant is quite complicated. But in somewhat simplified fashion we may say that we call a consonant **voiced**, if the vocal cords vibrate throughout the production of the sound, while we consider a consonant as **unvoiced** if throughout most or all of the production of the sound the vibration of the vocal cords is absent. On that basis we call the initial sound of English bin voiced, while of pin is unvoiced; the initial sound of English father is unvoiced, and that of veal is voiced.

The second criterion for the classification of consonants considers the **manner of production**. We have already mentioned that in the production of consonants the air stream meets an obstacle. If during the production of the sound the air stream is actually completely interrupted we call the sound a **stop**: a stop, then, is a sound which is produced by the act of closing and opening the path taken by the air during sound production. In this process of opening and closing, the air is often allowed to build up pressure against the obstacle and is then permitted to escape suddenly when the obstacle is removed. Stop sounds are also frequently referred to as **plosives**. The initial sounds of the English pick, tin, can, get, et cetera, are all plosive or stop sounds.

All sounds produced without any complete stoppage of the air stream are called **continuants** (vowels too are, therefore, continuants in the strict sense). Among the consonants we can distinguish different types of continuants. One important type is the **fricative**. In the production of the fricative the air stream meets an obstacle; there is no complete closure, but rather a constriction of the speech organs and throughout the production of the sounds the air is allowed to pass through the constriction. The initial sounds of the English father, veal, thin, this, sin, ship, are all fricative sounds, produced with air friction as they pass through a constriction of the vocal apparatus.

In case of another group of consonants, there is no real narrow constriction of the speech organs, but a modification or narrowing of the speech tract at one point or another during the production of the sound. These consonants are called **resonants** and the initial sounds of the English man, news, lion, ran, water, are examples of the resonants. In the case of the initial sounds in man, neat, or the final sound in song, the passage through the mouth is closed, but the passage through the nose is opened. It is for this reason that these resonants are also called **nasals**. In the case of [l], as in lion, the aperture is also closed by the contact that the tongue makes against the upper gum, although the air is allowed to escape freely at both sides of the tongue. The resonants produced in such a manner are called **laterals**. From the way we have characterized resonant consonants (absence or presence of any stoppage or even real constriction), it is also quite clear that in fact there is little absolute difference in kind between resonant consonants and vowels. As a matter of fact, vowels may be classified as resonants and the distinction between vowel and consonant—sharp and obvious if we compare vowels with stops or even fricatives—becomes blurred in the case of the resonant sounds and is difficult to make with any real precision. From the strictly phonetic point of view it is therefore a fairly arbitrary distinction.

Before leaving the discussion of the manner of production one more type of sound must be introduced: when producing a stop sound like the [t] in tin, the air stream is released suddenly after a brief stoppage. When, on the other hand, the obstacle is removed quite slowly, the air, instead of escaping with the explosion of the plosive, is allowed to pass over the obstacle more gradually. The result is that a fricative type of sound is produced. Instead of [t] as in tin, we get a sound that resembles [t] followed by [ʃ] as for instance in chin. This kind of sound, a stop with a slow release, is called an **affricate**.

The next comment concerns the sound [s] itself: how does it, for instance, differ from the initial sound of thin [θ] with which so many speakers of foreign languages, such as Frenchmen or Germans, are apt to confuse it? For one thing, [s] is produced with the tip of the tongue in a different position than in the case of [θ]. This is not the main difference however. Both [s] and [θ] are also fricative sounds. This means that the air is creating friction as it passes through a narrow opening, but the shape of the opening is different for the two sounds, for [θ] (just as, for instance, for [f] and [v]) the opening is wide from side to side and narrow from top to bottom. Such sounds are called **slit-fricatives**. For *s* the opening is narrow from side to side and deep from top to bottom: [s] is called a **groove fricative**. The consonant sounds corresponding to the boldface letters in plea**s**ure [ʒ] or **sh**ine [ʃ] or ro**s**e [z] are all groove fricatives. Since the grooved kind of opening results in those sounds having a hissing quality, they are also frequently called **sibilants**.

As far as the manner of articulation is concerned, two more types must be considered: the **trill** or **vibrant** sound, and the **flap**. The latter is produced by a single rapid movement of an articulator. It may be compared to a very short stop sound: the [r] of Spanish *pero* is such a flap. For the French student, however, the trill or vibrant category is more important. A vibrant consists of the very rapid alternation of sounds produced by the vibration of a flexible speech organ. The Southern French [r] is produced by the vibration of the tip of the tongue, and the [r] of standard French is produced by the vibration of the uvula.

Now the third criterion in consonant classification: this one concerns the place of stoppage of the air stream, or of maximum constriction of the speech organs: the **point of articulation**. The main classification proceeds according to the lower articulator used in the production of the sound, the lower of the speech organs which produce the stoppage or constriction. If this organ is the lower lip we call the sound **labial**; if it is the tip of the tongue (the apex) the sound is called **apical**; if it is the front of the tongue the sound is a **frontal**; if it is the back of the tongue (the dorsum), the sound is called **dorsal**. Thus, the initial sound of pin is a labial, that of tin is an apical, that of chin is a frontal, that of kin is classified as a dorsal. For most purposes this general classification according to the lower articulator is not precise enough. Therefore the usual classification considers the lower as well as the upper articulator. The following table summarizes the more precise classification according to both articulators involved.

Lower Articulator	Upper Articulator	Name of Sound
lower lip	upper lip	1. bilabial
lower lip	upper teeth	2. labio-dental
tip of tongue	teeth	3. dental
tip of tongue	gums of upper teeth (alveolae)	4. alveolar
tip of tongue (curled back against the palate)	palate	5. retroflex
front of tongue	gums of upper teeth (alveolae)	6. alveo-palatal
front of tongue	front of palate	7. prepalatal
back of tongue	back of palate	8. palatal
back of tongue	velum (soft palate)	9. veiar
back of tongue	uvula (back of velum)	10. uvular

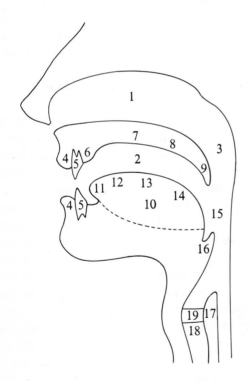

1. Nasal Cavity
2. Oral Cavity
3. Nasal passage
4. Lips
5. Teeth
6. Alveole
7. Hard Palate
8. Soft Palate
9. Uvula
10. Tongue
11. Tip of Tongue
12. Front of Tongue
13. Middle of Tongue
14. Back of Tongue
15. Pharynx
16. Epiglottis
17. Glottis
18. Larynx
19. Vocal Cords

Most of these points of articulation can be easily demonstrated by English sounds. Initial sounds of the following words may serve as illustration. Note how the point of articulation shifts back as you say the following:

> pin
> fin
> thin
> tin
> red
> chin
> yet
> kin
> cot
> (French: *rien*)

It is, of course, possible to produce sounds which have their point of articulation even farther back than the uvula, namely the larynx. Thus we can produce a stop just by the closure and opening of the vocal cords. This sound, a glottal stop (symbol ?), is produced in some languages (German and to a somewhat lesser degreee English) before any word beginning with a vowel sound. Some speakers of English, especially along the Eastern Seaboard such as New York and New Jersey, say a glottal stop in a word like bottle [ba?l]. A **fricative glottal sound** is produced if the air stream is allowed to pass through the constriction created between the vocal cords without any further modification taking place in the rest of the speech tract: the [h] sound of have, and her is such a **glottal fricative**.

Before summarizing our discussion of consonants, brief mention must be made of concomitant or secondary features: certain types of articulation which may accompany the articulation of a consonant. Thus the raising of the middle of the tongue against the palate may accompany the articulation of a consonant, which is then "palatalized". Or a rounding of the lips may take place while a dental or velar stop is pronounced, thus "labializing" that stop: for instance, the initial sound of English quick [kwɪk] can be interpreted as a **labialized stop**. The **aspiration** of a stop may also be an important accompanying feature: if after the release of a stop, air pressure is allowed to build up immediately (and before the production of the following vowel) a glottal fricative [h] will be heard between the stop and that vowel. This is normally the case in languages like English or German in which most stops are aspirated. On the other hand, if after the stop the buildup of air pressure is delayed until the production of the following vowel, the stop will be unaspirated as in French and the other Romance languages. The main differences between the initial sounds of English pin and French *pire* is, of course, the lack of aspiration of the French sound.

What we have reviewed here may seem a rather formidable array of terminology. Of course there is no need for the student ever to hear it. The teacher, on the other hand, may find it quite useful to know the terminology of phonetics. Some control of this nomenclature is needed to follow pedagogically important discussion in professional journals: even more important, the control of the nomenclature implies a basic understanding of how sounds are produced. There is obviously no point in memorizing that "the English [t] is an alveolar unvoiced stop." The real point is that for the one who understands the nomenclature, it gives in precise fashion the information about the pronunciation of English [t]. Once that person knows how English [t] is pronounced he has no need to memorize the nomenclature which is actually nothing but a condensed description of the pronunciation of the sound.

With this in mind let us review with the help of the table on page 58 the terminology we have learned so far. In it the points of articulation are given at the left in such a way that we move from the lips back as we proceed down the table. The manners of articulation are distinguished at the top of the table, and so is the contrast of voiced vs. unvoiced. Examples are taken from English with written symbols representing the sounds underlined.

We have already stated that the transition from consonant to vowel is really a gradual one. There is a group of sounds which are borderline cases and which are, therefore, classified as either **semi-consonants** or **semi-vowels**. For instance, the initial sound of the English water [w] is a **labial semi-vowel**, produced with a rounding of the lips. The initial sound of the English yes [j] in which the maximum construction occurs between the front of the tongue and the gums is classified as an **alveo-palatal semi-vowel**. English **r** as in red, for which the tip of the tongue is curled back and raised against the gums or palate may be classified as an **alveolar** or **retroflex semi-vowel.**

Since vowels proper are all voiced and produced without any major obstacle to the air stream, their method of classification is different from that of consonants. The nature of any vowel depends on various factors, such as the position of the tongue, the position (front or back)

Manner Points	STOPS		AFRICATES		FRICATIVES				RESONANTS	
					slit		*groove*		*lateral*	*nasal*
	voiced	*unvoiced*	*voiced*	*unvoiced*	*voiced*	*unvoiced*	*voiced*	*unvoiced*		
Bilabial	b (bin)	p (pin)								m (man)
Labio-dental					v (vat)	f (fat)				
Dental					ð (then)	θ (thin)				
Alveolar	d (din)	t (tin)					z (zinc)	s (sink)	l (late)	n (no)
Alveo-palatal			dʒ (gin)	tʃ (chin)			ʒ (vision)	ʃ (nation)		
Velar	g (goat)	k (coat)								ŋ (sing)
Glottal								h (hat)		

of the highest point of the tongue, the position of the lips, the aperture of the nasal passage. All of these modify the mouth resonator in different ways to produce vowels of varying qualities, whose possible number is almost unlimited. In order to classify vowels, phoneticians have, therefore, had recourse to the system of the cardinal vowels. These cardinal vowels do not really exist as such in any language. They are sounds which can be produced by the tongue in certain well-defined positions. Other vowels actually existing in living languages may then be defined in relation to these "theoretical" cardinal vowels. It so happens, however, that the French vowels are so near the cardinal vowels that we may actually use them to illustrate the cardinal vowels that we shall describe. If we raise the tongue as much as possible, and push it forward as far as possible at the same time, we produce the sound [i] (French *pire*). If we keep the tongue as far front as possible but drop it a little lower, we produce the sound [a] (French *patte*). If we raise the tongue as much as possible but draw it back as far as we can, the sound produced is [u] (French *fou*). If we keep the tongue in the back of the mouth but drop

it as much as possible we say the vowel [ɑ] (French *pâte*). [i] and [u]
are the maximum high vowels and [a] and [ɑ] are the maximum low
vowels. Likewise, [i] is the maximum front vowel, and [u] the maximum
back vowel. Between these four cardinal vowels, four more can be
established by interpolating two vowels between [i] and [a] in front and
[u] and [ɑ] in back, in such a way that they divide the distance between
the extreme high and low vowels into equal parts. The result is the following trapezoid, which is usually and somewhat inaccurately referred to
as the **cardinal vowel triangle**:

1. i (*pire*)	8. u (*fou*)
2. e (*les*)	7. o (*sot*)
3. ε (*père*)	6. ɔ (*sotte*)
4. a (*patte*)	5. ɑ (*pâte*)

We may again use French for examples of the **secondary cardinal
vowels**. In discussing the vowels we have so far paid no attention to
the position of the lips. We have simply assumed that our lips are spread
out wide when we produce front vowels like [i] (*pire*), [e] (*les*), et cetera,
and that they are rounded if we produce back vowels such as [u] (*fou*)
and [o] (*sot*). Actually, this combination of front and back vowels and
of lip position can be reversed. If we produce the front vowels with
rounded lips and the back vowels with spread lips, we can produce such
vowels sounds as described below:

1. [y]	8.
2. [ø]	7.
3. [œ]	6. [ʌ]
	5.

Only 1, 2, and 3, and to a lesser extent 6 are of importance to us.
There is no need for us to discuss or represent the vowels which should
appear next to the numbers 5, 7, and 8. [y] represents the vowel sound
of French *pur*, [ø] by the vowel of *peu*, [œ] by the vowel of peur. [ʌ] does
also occur in French being often the pronunciation of *o* in a word like
dommage.

Whereas in our discussion of consonants we were able to get our
examples from English, we had to turn to French to find examples for
our vowels. The reason for this is not only that French vowels are better
examples for the cardinal vowel system but also the fact that so many
English vowels are really **diphthongs**. This means that they are either
combinations of vowels and semi-vowels as in say [sεj] or that at any
rate they change their quality during the course of pronunciation.

We have now reviewed some of the major principles and concepts of phonetics. Before proceeding to a more detailed comparison of French and English sounds, we have to define one more concept, namely the **phoneme**.

(B) PHONEMICS

In terms of the analogy of language as a set of building stones, the phoneme may simply be defined as the smallest building stone available to the speaker of a particular language. Any language consists basically of a set (usually between 25 and 45) of building stones which may be used again and again, and recombined in different ways in order to form the more complex elements of the language. Thus, if a speaker of English says cat, he has combined the building stones /kæt/ to form a word. If he says /kit/ he has replaced one sound of these building stones and by doing so formed another word. The mere fact that he is able to do this proves that /æ/ and /ɪ/ are indeed **phonemes**, that is, the minimal building stones of the English language. Words like cat or kit which are differentiated only by one building stone are called **minimal pairs**. If two sounds differentiate a minimal pair, we have the best proof that they are phonemes of a given language: hence the fact that *roue* is one word and *rue* another proves that the sounds /u/ and /y/ are phonemes of French. (Following the generally accepted convention, we shall put phonemic transcription between slanted brackets / /. In other words, if we talk about sounds as such, we use [ ]; if we think of these sounds as building stones of a particular language, we use the slants / . . . /.)

The native speaker of any language is trained from childhood to perceive the differences between the phonemes of his language. After all, his language operates ultimately only through these differences. What makes *roue* and *rue* different words is the difference between /u/ and /y/. What makes *roue* and *loup* different words is the difference between /R/ and /l/. What makes the comprehension and pronunciation of foreign languages difficult is that our entire mechanism of comprehension and pronunciation is geared to perceive and differentiate the phonemic differences of our own language. The difference between *roue* and *rue* which is obvious to any Frenchman is often difficult for the speakers of English to hear, since English has no sound /y/ and does not, therefore, distinguish /u/ and /y/. Conversely, the difference between sin and sing is difficult to perceive for many Frenchmen since French has no sound /ŋ/ as in sing /sɪŋ/ and, obviously, does not distinguish /n/ and /ŋ/.

When a speaker of English says kid, he uses the building stone /k/ as initial sound of the word. If he says can /kæn/ or could /kʊd/ he again uses the same building stone as initial consonant. But the /k/ sounds in kid, could or can are not really identical. Even though they represent the same building stone of the English system, the exact shape of the building stone varies according to the vowel which follows the /k/ sound. The /k/ of /kɪd/ is pronounced much farther front than the /k/ of can, which in turn has a different point of articulation than the /k/ of could which is pronounced farther back than either of the two other /k/ sounds. In a similar way, we can observe that the sound /k/ in kin is really different from the /k/ of skin or the /k/ of beak. The /k/ of kin is followed by a puff of air—it is aspirated; the /k/ of skin is not. The /k/ of beak is again unlike the two others mentioned, insofar as it is usually "unreleased," that is, the airstream does not escape with an audible explosion; the sound is, so to speak, only half-finished. Now all the /k/ sounds which we have described are just variants of the same building stone /k/. We call them **positional variants** or **allophones** of the same phoneme. The difference between the /k/ of kit and the /k/ of skit depends entirely on the environment, in which they occur. The /k/ of kit occurs initially before vowels, the /k/ of skit occurs only after /s/. The first occurs only in a position in which the other one does not occur. The positions in which they appear are mutually exclusive or, to use technical terminology, these two variants of /k/ are in **complementary distribution.**

Since the use of the various types of /k/ just discussed depends on their environment and is predictable from their environment, it follows that differences between these various /k/ sounds could not be utilized to distinguish meaning in English. In other words, it would be impossible to find in English a minimal pair which was distinguished only by the difference between two types of /k/ sounds. There are, of course, languages in which different types of /k/ sounds are different phonemes. In such a language we might find a word like kʰa, with aspirated /k/, distinguished from a word ka, with unaspirated /k/. For native speakers of such a language the difference between these two /k/ sounds would be phonemic, and it would be as obvious to them as the difference between /p/ and /b/ or /t/ and /d/ is to a speaker of English. What is and what is not an obvious important sound distinction depends entirely on the system of a particular language.

The important contribution of phonemics to language teaching and especially to the teaching of pronunciation lies in the fact that it has simplified the task and systematized it. A speaker of any language produces an infinite variety of sounds as he speaks, but in doing so he is only using a fairly limited number of phonemes. Phonemic analysis teaches us to distinguish the unimportant from the important. We know that our student must be able to hear and produce the phonemic distinctions of French or he will neither be able to understand nor communicate. Phonemic analysis of French and English shows us quite clearly which of the French phonemes will be difficult to learn for speakers of English and must therefore be emphasized in our teaching. And finally, phonemics provides us with a real understanding of the psychological reasons for the "foreign accent." The reason lies not so much in the English speaker's inability to move his jaw muscles or tongue in the French way but rather in the fact that his whole system of auditory discrimination has been geared to the English phonemic differences. It is for this reason that he is apt to find it difficult to distinguish between certain French sounds. It is under the impact of phonemic theory that in the teaching of pronunciation our emphasis has been shifted to the teaching of auditory discrimination as the initial step. **A student must be able to hear and comprehend before he can be made to imitate and to speak.**

CHAPTER VI

Teaching Pronunciation

We shall now apply the concepts learned in the preceding chapter to the specific problem of teaching French pronunciation. We will proceed by comparing French and English consonants, vowels, and intonation patterns, and by discussing French orthography and pronunciation. Under each heading we shall try to summarize the major teaching problems and techniques which arise from our discussion. There are several excellent books dealing with such subjects as English phonemics and French pronunciation. Our purpose will therefore be to focus our attention on the points with which every teacher should be familiar rather than to give an exhaustive treatment.

In reading the discussion of teaching techniques, it should be kept in mind that we are thinking primarily of the Senior High School and College level. Ultimately the acquisition of a good pronunciation by the student depends on a good pronunciation on the part of the teacher and his insistence on accurate (or at least increasingly accurate) repetition by the student. On the Junior High School and certainly the elementary school level, these are probably the main requisites of the teaching of pronunciation.

(A) CONSONANTS

Let us start by simply listing the consonant phonemes of French. For each phoneme we shall give the phonetic symbol and a sample word in which the letter corresponding to the sound will be **in bold type**.

/p/	*pas*	/f/	*fou*	/m/	*mon*
/b/	*bas*	/v/	*vous*	/n/	*non*

/t/	*ton*	/s/	*sont*	/ɲ/	*agneau*
/d/	*don*	/z/	*vase*	/l/	*loup*
/k/	*cas*	/ʃ/	*chez*	/ʀ/	*roue*
/g/	*gare*	/ʒ/	*je*		

In addition, French has three semivowels which can be conveniently grouped with the consonants

/w/ *Louis*   /ɥ/ *lui*   /j/ *fille*

We can now arrange these consonants according to the criteria of classification (**manner and point of articulation; voiced vs. unvoiced**) discussed in the previous chapter and compare them simultaneously with the list of English consonants:

	Bilabial	Labio-Dental	Dental	Alveolar	Alveo-Palatal	Velar	Uvular
FRENCH stop	p, b		t, d			k, g	
fricative: slit groove		f, v		s, z	ʃ ʒ		
lateral			l				
vibrant						R	(R)
nasal	m		n		ɲ		
semi-vowels	w				j, ɥ		
ENGLISH stop	p, b			t, d	tʃ dʒ	k, g	
fricative: slit groove		f, v	θ, ð s, z		ʃ ʒ	(glottal: h)	
lateral				l			
nasal	m			n		ŋ	
semi-vowels	w			r	j		

A comparison of the English and French tables points out quite clearly some important facts: first of all, when it comes to the pronunciation of consonants, the Frenchman hearing English will probably have more difficulty than the American hearing French. The Frenchman will have to learn the sounds /tʃ/ as in chin, /dʒ/ as in gin, /θ/ as in thin, /ð/ as in those, /ŋ/ as in sing, and /h/ as in have, all of which are completely foreign to his system, since they do not have any French counterpart. The French speaker will probably have quite a problem in mastering the auditory discrimination between those sounds and other sounds of the English system (such as thin vs. sin; sing vs. sin). The American student has to learn only two completely new sounds: /ɲ/ as in *agneau* and /ɥ/ as in *lui*. Within the French consonant system he has therefore no major problem of auditory discrimination. His problem will be almost entirely in the substitution of English sounds for French sounds.

The sound /ɲ/ is comparatively easy to learn: it is produced with the tip of the tongue against the lower gums and the back of the tongue raised against the palate. The tongue position is thus very similar to the one of the /j/ in English yes or in French *fille*; but as in any nasal sound, the air is forced out through the nasal passage. Several textbooks describe the sound as a combination of /n/ + /j/ and compare it to the sound produced in English onion. This is close to the fact. It is a single sound, not a combination of two, and the sound produced in "onion" is a reasonably close approximation.

The other "completely new sound" mentioned thus far, /ɥ/, provides the one example of an auditory discrimination problem which speakers of English are likely to encounter with French consonants or semivowels: they may have difficulties with the contrast between /w/ and /ɥ/. The best way of establishing auditory discrimination is through the contrast of minimal pairs, in other words utterances which are distinguished by the contrast alone and which allow the student to concentrate on the one feature which presents difficulty. The student must be trained to hear the contrast between *lui* /lɥi/ and *Louis* /lwi/; *juin* /ʒɥɛ̃/ and *joint* /ʒwɛ̃/, et cetera. The teacher may pronounce these words and ask the student to repeat them. He can then assign a number (*juin* = 1; *joint* = 2) to each word, ask the student to identify whether he is pronouncing 1 or 2. The teacher may also pronounce one of the words (*juin*) and then after a short pause, a short sequence made up of the words of the minimal pair (*joint-juin-joint*), and ask the student to indicate which of the words pronounced after the pause was a repetition of the word which preceded the pause. He may also pronounce a sequence like *joint-juin-joint* and ask the student simply to identify which of the words were the same, or which one was different from the rest.

As in all such cases the establishment of auditory discrimination is only the initial step; for most individuals it must be followed by a description of sound production. The /ɥ/ of *lui* is distinguished from the /w/ of *Louis* through the position of the lips and tongue: the lips are less rounded than in /w/ and the tongue is pressed forward and not backward. In the production of /ɥ/ the speech organs move briefly forward as for /y/ as in *lu*. Once the student has mastered the /y/ sound (see discussion of vowels below), he usually has no trouble with /ɥ/.

Sounds which have some sort of counterpart in the native language of the learner are not necessarily easy to learn. Sometimes they are more difficult than the completely new sounds, because with the similar sounds the interference of the native language is apt to be even greater than with the completely new ones. French /ʀ/ is a good case in point. Its actual similarity to English /r/ is slight. They are both continuants, but we classified the English /r/ as a semivowel: most English speakers produce it with the tip of the tongue near the alveolar area and slightly rounded lips. There may be variations of this pronunciation but they are all still quite different from the French /ʀ/. In the production of the latter, the lips and the front of the tongue play no part whatsoever. There are several ways of saying a French /ʀ/. The two most frequent are: (1) by the friction of the air stream against the uvula or (2) by the friction created as the air stream passes between the very back part of the tongue and the velum. The tongue position for the French /ʀ/ is thus similar to the one for /g/. The student can thus be told to pronounce [ga] and then to release slightly the closure of [g] and let the air go through the passage thus created in back of the mouth, so that the sound may shift to [ʀa]. Another articulatory recipe involves the starting position of [ɑ] as in the English father, or the French *bas*. From the position of [ɑ] the student can then try to reach the French /ʀ/ by keeping the front of the tongue and lips in the [ɑ] position and by slightly lowering the velum and raising the back of his tongue. Another well-known recipe for the production of the uvular French [ʀ] sound is the advice to imitate the sound produced by gargling.

French /ʀ/ and English /r/ are so different that auditory discrimination between the two sounds is not a major factor in the learning process. This is not the situation with the other French consonant sounds which have very close English counterparts. We have already mentioned that English /k/ has three major variants: initial before vowel is aspirated (as in kin); after /s/ it is unaspirated (as in skin); at the end of the word it is "unreleased" (as in beak). The other English unvoiced stops /t/

and /p/ behave similarly. Thus /t/ or /p/ in tin or pin is aspirated; they are unaspirated in steam or spin; unreleased in get or step.

The /t/, /p/, and /k/ of French are always unaspirated and fully released. This means that only English /p/, /t/, /k/ as they occur after /s/ can be good substitutes for the French sounds. One possible way of teaching the pronunciation of French /p/, /t/, /k/ is then to tell the student to try to produce the French sounds like the variants he usually produces after /s/ and to say the stops in French *type*, *pas*, et cetera, as if they had been preceded by an /s/. Unfortunately, this does not always work for the student, since most speakers of English are quite unaware of the difference in pronunciation of the unvoiced stops after /s/ and in other positions. Auditory discrimination between the aspirated and unaspirated stops must therefore be developed. A newly developed technique to show the difference between English and French sounds which has appeared recently in several textbooks is to contrast French and English words which sound similar. This method can be employed in the classroom by a teacher who has a reasonably good French pronunciation; it can be done even more profitably in the language laboratory through the use of a tape recorded by a bilingual English–French speaker. The difference between the aspirated stops of English and the unaspirated stops of French can thus be made clear to the student by contrasting for him pairs like English peak and French *pique*, English tell and French *tel*, English key and French *qui*. The difference between the released stops of French and the unreleased of English is demonstrated by French *type* vs. English tip, French *patte* vs. English pot, French *lac* vs. English lock. One might say that this method employs the pedagogical advantage of the minimal pair concept on an interlingual basis: it does not give the contrast between the phonemes of the same language, but the difference between sounds of different languages which are presented to the student in isolation.

English and French /t/ differ not only in the matter of aspiration. Related to this difference is also the fact that English /t/ is **alveolar** (tip of the tongue against the alveolar ridge of the upper teeth), while French /t/ is **dental** (tip of tongue against back of teeth). From our comparative chart we see that this particular difference between English and French articulation holds true also for the sounds /d/, /l/, and /n/. The English sounds are all produced with the concave tongue pointing to the upper gums, whereas the French sounds are produced with the convex tongue pointing at the teeth. This basic difference in articulation should be observed not only because it makes some difference in the pronunciation of the consonants themselves, but also because it affects the pronunciation of the following vowels. As far as the consonants themselves are concerned, it makes French /l/, in particular, sound quite different from the English /l/. In *loup*, and *lac*, the /l/ sound has a different quality from that of English *Lou* and *lock*. English and French /ʃ/ and /ʒ/ are also produced somewhat differently. French /ʃ/ and /ʒ/ as in *chaîne* and *général* are produced with the front of tongue against the alveolar ridge; in the English sounds the tongue is again concave and the tip is pointed to the alveolar ridge. There is little difference in the sounds themselves, but the English tongue position makes it difficult to give the correct French pronunciation to the following vowel. Some students also have difficulty with the French /ʒ/ as in *général* in initial position, perhaps because the /ʒ/ phoneme of English as in measure, pleasure, garage, does not occur initially. They substitute the affricate /dʒ/ as in general which does occur initially in English. It is also possible that this particular mistake is due to the influence of the English orthography (g(e) = dʒ) rather than to a genuine interference of the sound system.

French /f/, /v/, /m/, /j/, /b/, and /g/ are close enough to their English counterparts so that they do not merit special discussions. What remains for us to point out in the comparison of English and French consonant phonemes is that positional variations (allophones) are generally more important in English than in French. We have already seen how different positions affect the pronunciation of unvoiced stops. Something similar is true in the pronunciation of the voiced sounds /b/, /d/, /g/, /l/. In English bad, good, tell, the last consonants sound quite different from the way they do at the beginning of the word: they lose their voicing before they are half through. If they are stops, they are unreleased, or half-finished. The American student should be careful not to carry these allophones into his French. The French sounds are in no way different from the way they are in initial position: the last consonants of words like *tel*/tɛl/, *digue*/dig/, and *belle*/bɛl/ are fully pronounced. Thus the pronunciation of such words can be contrasted with English words like tell, dig, bell, so that the student can be made fully aware of the difference.

Other positional modifications of English consonants which are particularly obnoxious if they are imported into French pronunciation concern /r/ and /l/ in preconsonantal and final position. These modifications vary considerably from one American dialect to another, and affect also the pronunciation of the preceding vowel. Thus the final

/r/ is dropped and transformed into a vowel glide in parts of the Eastern and Southern U.S. In other parts of the United States, there is a glide between the /r/ and the vowel, and the /r/ is preserved in a "half-pronounced" manner. Both /r/ and /l/ cause glides and in some parts of the United States disappear completely before other consonants. But no matter what part of the United States a student may come from, he should not import his pronunciation of /l/ of /r/ as in halt, arm, car, dear, into French. If he does make this particular mistake, the contrast between these English words and such French words as *halte*, *arme*, *car*, *dire*, might be pointed out to him as a preliminary step to the drill of the correct French pronunciation in repetition exercises.

(B) VOWELS

In our discussion of general phonetic terminology we used French rather than English vowels as illustration, because the English vowel system is rather complex. Different linguists have advanced different interpretations of the English vowel system. There is no need for the French teacher to understand the exact differences and problems involved in those interpretations. The principles involved are, however, important. Many English vowels are, in fact, diphthongs: if we say bee, we can note quite easily how the vowel corresponding to the ee glides upward during its production. What we are saying in fact is something like /ɪj/. If we say food, we can observe again how during the production of the vowel the sound changes; the tongue moves up and backward and the lips become more rounded as we approach the end of the sound, which may be transcribed as /ʊw/. Starting with these considerations, some linguists have concluded that the vowel in words like bee, beat, see, or the vowel in do, shoe, is in fact not just one building stone, but two: bee is not /bi/ but /bɪj/; food is not /fud/ but /fʊwd/. To be more specific, the vowel of bee is then composed of a variant of the same vowel that is pronounced in bit plus a postvocalic variant of the same /j/ that occurs in the first sound of yes. The vowel of food is composed of a variant of the vowel of good plus a postvocalic variant of the same /w/ that begins the word water.

Other linguists have thought that they have found yet a third postvocalic vowel glide that is in fact a variant of a phoneme. Comparing the way words like cot and caught are pronounced (in some dialects at least), they felt that the difference between the two lies in the fact that the vowel of the second word is followed by a sort of neutral, voiceless glide which they interpret as the postvocalic variant of the sound /h/ of have, here.

It may be seen that the complexities and difficulties of English phonemics deal basically with one problem, whether to interpret some of the English diphthongs as one phoneme or as a combination of two. If we interpret the diphthongs as one phoneme, then the vowels of bet /bɛt/ and bait /bet/ are two different phonemes. If we interpret them as two, the vowels of bait consist of the same phoneme as in the vowel of bet, followed by the postvocalic variant of /j/, hence /bɛt/ vs. /bɛjt/. This type of interpretation is found in several textbooks. The teacher using such books should understand the basic principle underlying this interpretation. From the pedagogical viewpoint, the most important fact to retain is the diphthongal nature of the vowels and the existence of various glides which appear in English between vowel and following consonant. The exact phonemic interpretation of these glides varies from linguist to linguist and dialect to dialect.

For the purpose of illustrating the differences between English and French vowels, the following somewhat simplified scheme, which considers the diphthongs as unit phonemes, is probably easier to handle:

English Vowels

/i/ beat			/u/ food	
/ɪ/ bit			/ʊ/ good	
/e/ bait	/ə/ (but)		/o/ boat	
/ɛ/ bet			/ɔ/ bought	
/æ/ bat				
		hot /ɑ/		

The preceding scheme is valid for large areas of the Middle West of the United States. For other areas some of the sample words do not fit. For instance, the pronunciation of hot in New England does not illustrate the /ɑ/ sound, and a word like father might be a better example for the sound in that area.

The following table illustrates the French vowel phonemes:

/i/ *plie*	/y/ *pur*		/u/ *doux*
/e/ *les*	/ø/ *peu*	/ə/ *le*	/o/ *peau*
/ɛ/ *même*	/œ/ *peur*		/ɔ/ *note*
/a/ *car*			/ɑ/ *bas*

In addition, the sounds /ɛ/, /ɑ/, /ɔ/, /œ/ occur also in nasalized form: /ɛ̃/ as in *vin,* /ɑ̃/ as in *an,* /ɔ̃/ as in *on* and /œ̃/ as in *un.*

We must, of course, keep in mind that no French vowel is really exactly like any English vowel. French vowels are produced with much more tension in the speech organs than English vowels. But leaving aside for the time being some of the details of the French system, the comparison with English brings out the very obvious fact that the French sounds /y/, /œ/, /ø/ and the nasals /ɛ̃/, /ɔ̃/, /ɑ̃/, /œ̃/ have no possible counterparts in the English system. They offer serious problems in production and sometimes in auditory discrimination to the American student.

The auditory discrimination problem can be tackled by the method of training discrimination between minimal pairs. The vowels /y/, /ø/, /œ/ should be contrasted among themselves: /y/œ/: *pur/peur, sur/soeur, mur/meurt*; /y/ø/: *pu/peu, du/deux*, fut/feu; /y/, /œ/ and /ø/ should also be contrasted with the corresponding back vowels: /ø/o/: *deux/dos, peut/peau, veut/vaut*; /œ/ɔ/: *leur/l'or, meurt/mort, soeur/sort*. Especially the contrast /y/u must be drilled very carefully, since for many Americans the sound /u/ is the favorite substitute for /y/. The instructor must emphasize contrasts like *roue/rue, doux/du, loup/lu, sou/su*.

The nasal vowels must also be contrasted among themselves: /ɑ̃/ɔ̃/: *dans/don, ment/mon, vend/vont*; /ɑ̃/ɛ̃/: *vent/vingt, sent/sein, temps/teint*; /ɔ̃/ɛ̃/: *bon/bain, ton/teint, vont/vin*. In connection with the auditory discrimination between nasal vowels, it is interesting to note that many native French speakers no longer distinguish /œ̃/ from /ɛ̃/, but use the latter for both. Under these circumstances it is probably not profitable to spend too much time teaching this contrast to the beginning American student. Special care must be taken, however, to teach the nasal and non-nasal contrast. American students have considerable difficulty distinguishing *côte* from *conte*, or even *beau* from *bon*. The reason for this is simple: nasality also exists in English. Vowels following or preceding a nasal consonant (such as no, down) are nasalized, but since this nasality in English is only the result of the consonant and has no phonemic significance, speakers of English are not used to paying attention to the nasal pronunciation of the vowel.

As far as the articulation of /y/, /ø/, /œ/ is concerned, the problem is, of course, to teach American students to combine the tongue position of /i/, /e/, /ɛ/ with the lip rounding which they are used to only in the pronunciation of the back vowels. Thus the student may be asked to pronounce /i/ as in *li* or *ri*, and then to round his lips and push them as far forward as possible to get to the correct pronunciation of *lu* or *rue*. Since the speaker of English is not used to lip rounding and the *i* position as simultaneous components of a sound, many students will try to do the one after the other: instead of French /y/ they will then say something like /ju/, that is, they will pronounce French *du* like English due. The approach to teaching of /ø/ and /oe/ is analogous to that of teaching /y/: we start with words like père and fée, and get the student to reach the /ø/ and /oe/ sounds by keeping the tongue position and moving his rounded lips forward: père → peur; fée → feu.

The pronunciation of the nasal vowels is best approached through their non-nasal counterparts. The vowels of *ta, vais, peau* (/a/, /ɛ/, /o/) are produced with approximately the same tongue position as those of *tant* /ã/ *vin* /vɛ̃/ and *pont* /pɔ̃/. What the student must learn is to push the air through the nasal passages as he shifts from *vais* to *vingt*, *tait* to *teint*, *dos* to *dont*, *va* to *vend*. The major mistakes the American students are apt to make are: (1) to diphthongize the nasal—in other words, say something like /dawn/ or *down* instead of /dã/ and /dɔ̃/; (2) to produce nasal consonants after the nasal vowel /dõn/ or possibly /down/ instead of /dɔ̃/. The reason for the latter mistake follows from what we have said about nasal vowels in English. Since vowel nasality in English occurs in conjunction with nasal consonants (ample, down), the American student needs the crutch of the nasal consonant in order to produce the vowel. In French the situation is of course the reverse: with rare exceptions, nasal vowels are not followed by pronounced nasal consonants (*ancien* /ãsjɛ̃/; *bon* /bɔ̃/), and if the nasal consonant is pronounced, the preceding vowel is usually clear from any nasality (*bonne* /bɔn/, *ancienne* /ãsjɛn/). The American student with his tendency to produce nasal vowels followed by nasal consonants is apt to blur the differences between *bon* /bɔ̃/ and *bonne* /bɔn/; *son* /sɔ̃/ and *sonne* /sɔn/; *Jean* /ʒã/ and *Jeanne* /ʒan/. Special auditory discrimination and pronunciation exercises, and contrasting pairs such as those mentioned above, are of great help in this situation.

The French vowels not yet discussed are those which have reasonably close counterparts in the English system. It is, of course, precisely the substitution of these counterparts which must be avoided. In the case of the vowels /ɛ/ (*même, dette*) and /ɔ/ (*botte, folle*), the substitution of the English vowels /ɛ/ (bet, set) and /ɔ/ (fork, bought) is less obnoxious to the French ear than other kinds of substitutions. The English and French vowels are fairly close to each other, the main difference being the greater tenseness of the French sounds.

The substitution of English vowels for French /i/, /e/, /u/, /o/ on the other hand is a rather serious and noticeable mistake. English has two

sounds (bit, beat) which the student is apt to substitute for the French
/i/. The /ɪ/ of bit is too low, the /i/ of beat is, as we have pointed out
before, really a diphthong /ɪj/. Neither of these sounds is an acceptable
substitute for the very high, nondiphthongal French /i/. In the case of
the French /u/ the state of affairs is quite similar. The /ʊ/ of English
good is too low, the /u/ of food or do is a diphthongal /ʊw/. As far
as French /o/ and /e/ are concerned, the corresponding English sound
in boat, bone, and gate, gay, are also diphthongs and quite unacceptable
to the French ear.

The first attack on the problem is to develop the student's auditory
discrimination between the English and French sounds. This may be
done again by contrasting English and French words which sound
almost alike and present the English and French sound contrasts in
quasi-isolation:

English i/French *i*: key/*qui*; peak/*pique*; sea/*si*
English ɪ/French *i*: pick/*pique*; kit/*quitte*; click/*clique*
English u/French *u*: do/*doux*; fool/*foule*; pool/*poule*
English ʊ/French *u*: pull/*poule*; full/*foule*
English o/French *o*: foe/*faut*; toe/*tôt*; so/*sot*
English e/French *e*: say/*ses*; gay/*gai*; may/*mes*

Drills based on word contrasts such as the above might include
asking the student to pick out the French word in a series like key-
qui-key-key or the English word in *qui-qui*-key-*qui*. It is perhaps best
not to tell the student that actually English and French words are being
contrasted but to simply inform him that in a series like *qui-qui*-key-*qui*
he is to pick the instance in which French *qui* is pronounced with an
English accent. Exercises like this may then be used as dictation exercises
in which the student is asked to write down only words pronounced
accurately in French. The student's response to *qui*-key-*qui* will be
qui - - - *qui*. If this type of drill is used before the student is exposed
to French writing and orthography, he may be asked to write special
symbols in response to a correctly or incorrectly pronounced word. If
a series *qui*-key-*qui* were given, his response might then be + − +.

In the teaching of the actual articulation of the French /i/, /u/, /e/
and /o/ sounds it is necessary to remember that both /i/ and /u/ are
produced with tongue pushed as high up as possible and that also for
/e/ and /o/ the tongue is considerably higher than in the English counterparts. The lip rounding in French /u/ and /o/ is also much more pronounced than in the American /u/ and /o/ sounds.

This leaves French /ɑ/, /a/ and /ə/ to be discussed: /ɑ/ as in *bas*, *pâte* offers little difficulty. The /a/ of *pas* and *patte* is lower than the American /æ/ of bat, higher than the American /ɑ/ of Middle Western hot. Auditory discrimination exercises may again help the American student to recognize the French sound: *patte* contrasts with English pat as well as pot; the correct articulation depends primarily on the tenseness of the speech organs, and the right tongue position (between English /æ/ and /ɑ/ and lack of lip rounding in the pronunciation of the French sound.

The French /ə/ sound of *le*, *me*, *se*, et cetera, offers several problems. Some students will confuse it with the French /œ/ or /ø/. It is then necessary to contrast it with these sounds and to develop auditory comprehension between *les* and *le* (plural and singular), *des* and *de*, and between *je* and *jeu*, *je dis* and *jeudi*. As far as sound substitution is concerned, the English /ə/ of but is quite different from French /ə/, but the variety of /ə/ produced in the unaccented syllable of English word (regard -/rəgard/ support -/səpɔrt/) is quite similar. The main difference between the English and French vowel is that the French is tenser and produced with more rounded lips. The main difficulty is likely to be that the American student, used to producing his vowel only in an unstressed syllable, will carry his particular habits of stressing and unstressing syllables over into French in association with the /ə/ sound. This is a problem dealt with more fully in our discussion of French and English intonation.

In our discussion of French vowel phonemes we did not distinguish vowels according to their length. But all French vowels are not equally long. They are different, and with a few exceptions their length depends entirely on their environment. It is predictable and therefore, as is the absence of aspiration in English /p/ after /s/, nonphonemic. French vowels are short if they are followed in the same syllable by the consonants /p/, /t/, /k/ or groups such as /rp/, /rt/, /kt/, as in *type*, *rater*, *parte*, *lac*, *pacte*. They are long if they are nasal or followed by the consonants /r/, /z/, /ʒ/, /v/. In our phonetic transcription we can indicate this length by the sign [:] or a line over the vowel: rare [ʀɑ: ʀ] or [ʀɑ̄ʀ], *tige* [ti: ʒ], *neige* [nɛ: ʒ], *pense* [pɑ̃: s], *dont* [dɔ̃:], and so on. The third degree of length, which is between long and short and which we might call normal or average, is found in all other cases, before consonants like /b/, /g/, /d/, /m/, /n/, /j/, /ʃ/, as in *digue*, *robe*, *sale*, *femme*, *dame*, *riche*, and whenever the vowel is final in its syllable, as in *pris*, *voulu*, *lit*, *ami*, *donné*.

There are a few pairs of words which do contradict our above stated principle that the vowel length in French is nonphonemic and predictable. These are words which are distinguished by vowel length only: *mettre* /mɛtʀ/ vs. *maître* /mɛ: tʀ/, *belle* /bɛl/ vs. *bêle* /bɛ: l/, *vaine* /vɛn/ vs. *veine* /vɛ: n/. Such pairs are remnants—fossils, we might say— from a period when vowel length was utilized more widely in the language. The general trend is to dispense with vowel length as a significant feature. Thus distinctions like *belle* vs. *bêle* are generally no longer made in rapid colloquial speech.

In rapid colloquial speech the French vowel system undergoes certain other slight modifications: in rapid speech Frenchmen will generally not distinguish between words like *tache* /taʃ/ and *tâche* /tɑ: ʃ/ or *patte* /pat/ and *pâte* /pɑ: t/ *mal* /mal/ and *malle* /mɑ: l/. This means that the backvowel /ɑ/ may disappear as a separate phoneme of the language. In fact, in colloquial French /ø/ as opposed to /œ/, and /e/ as opposed to /ɛ/, also disappear as distinct phonemes of the language. This does not mean that the sounds as such disappear, but whether one says /ø/ or /œ/ or /e/ or /ɛ/ becomes clearly predictable according to the environment in which the sounds are used. /ø/ is used if the vowel is final in its syllable (in an open syllable) or if it is followed by /z/ in the same syllable; /œ/ is used whenever the vowel is followed by any other consonant (in a closed syllable). Thus we say *peu* /pø/ *heureux* /œRø/ or *heureuse* /œRøz/ but *peur* /pœR/ *seul* /sœl/, et cetera. In slow speech we distinguish *jeune* /ʒœn/ from *jeûne* /ʒø: n/ but in fast colloquial they both become /ʒœn/. The distribution of /e/ or /ɛ/ in fast colloquial speech follows a similar principle: /e/ is used whenever the vowel is an open syllable, /ɛ/ whenever it is in a closed syllable. Thus in rapid speech Frenchmen will pronounce *ferai* as /fre/, *ferais* also as /fre/, *étais* as /ete/, just like *été*, and use the sound /ɛ/ only in closed syllables: *même* /mɛm/, *dette* /dɛt/. Only in slow and more formal speech do they distinguish /e/ and /ɛ/ in open syllables: *dirai* /diRe/ with close *e*, but *dirais* /diRɛ/ with open /ɛ/.

We can thus formulate a general rule that, by and large, open vowels, /ɛ/, /œ/, /ɔ/, are used in closed syllables, while the close vowels, /e/, /ø/, /o/, are used in open syllables. The exceptions to this rule as far as /ɛ/: /e/ and /œ/: /ø/ are concerned have just been noted. In the case of /o/ vs. /ɔ/ the main exceptions are: (1) the use of /o/ rather than /ɔ/ before /z/, as in *rose* /ʀoz/, *chose* /ʃoz/, *ose* /oz/; (2) /o/ rather than /ɔ/ in several words in which the *o*-sound corresponds to the orthography *au*, as in *haute* /ot/ *fausse* /fos/, *jaune* /ʒon/; (3) and the use of

/ɔ/ regardless of the open or closed syllable if the /ɔ/ is not in the final syllable of the word: *philosophie* /filɔzɔfi/, *doctoral* /dɔktɔRal/, *porter* /pɔRte/, *potage* /pɔtaʒ/. Generally speaking, however, the use of /ɔ/ vs. /o/ does depend on the nature of the syllable: /o/ in open syllable: *les os* /lezo/, *sot* /so/, *peau* /po/; /ɔ/ in closed syllables: *l'os* /lɔs/, *sotte* /sɔt/, *porte* /pɔRt/.

The general principles affecting the use of /œ/, /ɔ/, /ɛ/ vs. /ø/, /o/, /e/ should be pointed out to students and they should note the difference in pronunciation of the vowel in words like *peu* /pø/ and *peur* /pœR/, or *jeune* /ʒœn/, and *jeu* /ʒø/, or *ses* /se/ and *cette* /sɛt/, and *oeuf* /œf/ and *oeufs* /ø/, *veut* /vø/ and *veulent* /vœl/. Since this change of pronunciation according to position usually involves a different phonetic response to the same orthographic symbols or a change of pronunciation of the root of a verb or adjective, many students are apt to confuse the open and close sounds unless they are specifically made aware of the difference and drilled in contrasts like *il peut* /ilpø/ vs. *ils peuvent* /il pœv/, or *premier* /pRəmje/ vs. *première* /pRəmjɛR/.

(C) ENGLISH AND FRENCH INTONATION

So far in our consideration of English and French phonemics we have been dealing with the small building blocks which are the smallest units of the two systems. But we all know that there is more to speech than just a succession of small building blocks. If we said a sentence like "He is coming" by just using one phoneme next to the other, we would be producing a lifeless, monotonous succession of sounds. But we do not talk like this. We vary the stress, and the pitch of our voice and the way in which we connect syllables. These ways of stressing, using pitch and connecting syllables are also an important part of the system of any language. As far as English is concerned, they have been studied and described by various linguists, in somewhat different forms and with certain disagreement as to detail. Yet the essentials of English intonation which the French teacher must be aware of are clear enough.

In any English word of two or more syllables, one syllable is stressed more heavily than the others: Énglish, Américan, sýllables. This stress is movable; the stress could fall on any syllable of the word, so we cannot predict which syllable will be stressed. However, if we stress the wrong sylláble (stress on the a), a native speaker will notice it immediately; moreover, it is also possible in English to make some nouns into verbs and vice versa simply by shifting the stress. Pérmit is a noun, permit is a verb. For this reason, we may say that the stress itself has the power of distinguishing meaning; that is, stress is a phoneme of English.

Most linguists agree that there are four different degrees of stress in English: the heaviest or the **primary stress** which may be exemplified by the stress in the above quoted pérmit: the absence of stress, or **weak stress**, as in the unstressed syllable of the above example. Between these two (primary and weak) there are two more possible levels of emphasis: one that may be exemplified by the degree of the stress in the first syllable of a word like liberation—not as strong as the primary stress on the a but stronger than the weak stress on -be or -tion. This is called the **tertiary stress**. The secondary stress can be illustrated by the comparison of such expressions as "White House" (the house of the United States President) and "white house" (any house that is painted white). In the first expression, White House is a unit, with the primary stress on white, and the tertiary stress on house. In the second expression, white and house are two separate units, with primary stress on house and secondary stress on white.

The difference between White House and white house may also serve to illustrate another peculiarity of English speech, namely the significant difference in the connection between syllables. The way in which white and house are linked obviously differs in the two expressions. In White House the syllables are linked quite closely; linguists call this way of connecting syllables **closed juncture**. In white house, the connection between the two syllables is not as direct, and we feel that there is some sort of marked interruption between the two: this kind of connection between syllables in English is referred to as **open juncture**. Pairs of expressions which are often quoted in textbooks to illustrate the two different junctures are night rate and nitrate, or a name and an aim: the difference between the two depends on the syllable connection, **juncture**. It is a difference that will be made and understood by speakers of English since it expresses quite clearly a difference in meaning. In other words the different types of juncture are phonemes of English. Quite typically (though not necessarily in all cases) the open juncture type of connection coincides with word boundaries.

As we speak we vary the degree of tension of our vocal cords. Just as on a violin we can produce a higher tone by tightening the strings and lower tones by loosening them, we change the quality of our voice by those variations of tension of the vocal cords. We change the **pitch** of our voice. These variations of pitch follow definite patterns which linguists have attempted to describe. As far as English is concerned, there is some agreement that there are four general levels or **registers of pitch** which can be used and which can express different meanings if they are used in different combinations and sequences: thus in a sentence like "He is going to New York today" (simple declarative statement) we start on the middle register and switch to the high register for the word York, and end the sentence in the low pitch.

He is going to New ⌐York⌐ today.

If, on the other hand, we start on the middle level, go to the high level on is, and finish the sentence on the low level

He ⌐is⌐ going to New York today.

we convey a meaning of affirmation. Or if we begin on the high level, shift immediately to the low level for the rest of the sentence

He⌐ is going to New York today.

we indicate that it is this person and no other, who is going to New York. From this, it is easy to see how various combinations of these levels or registers produce differences in the meaning conveyed by the sentence.

Perhaps the most essential points for the French teacher to remember are that: (1) in the English pitch system the high pitch is usually associated with the loudest stress (as in the example He is going to New York, mid-high-low), and that (2) the **transition** between two pitch levels of English can be made within the vowel sound. In a sentence like I am going home (simple declarative statement) we start on the medium level, go to the **high** level with the onset of the word home, and reach the **low** level by the time we finish the word.

Keeping in mind these general remarks on English stress, pitch, and juncture, let us approach the study of French intonation. French stress does not serve the distinctive phonemic function it has in English. By and large all the syllables of a French utterance receive the same amount of stress; there are only two major exceptions to this rule. (1) The last syllable of a word or stress group is normally pronounced with greater stress than the rest. This stressing of the last syllable of a word like *liberté* or a phrase like *Est-il arrivé?* usually amounts to a lengthening of the syllable rather than a really more emphatic pronunciation. At any rate, it is clearly predictable (that is, always occurs in the last syllable) and therefore useless from the point of view of expressing differences in meaning. (2) The other type of stress found in French expresses an emotional reaction of the speaker: it is the *accent d'intensité*, which can occur in a phrase like *C'est impossible!* or *Quelle impertinence!* It usually appears on the first or second syllable of the noun or adjective and is produced by an emphatic lengthening of the consonant rather than of the vowel.

One of the major problems of the speaker of English is to unlearn his English stressing habits when he is speaking French. How can he resist the temptation of stressing one syllable of a word at the expense of others? One possible way of teaching this is again to develop the auditory discrimination between the English and French habits. We can contrast French and English words which resemble each other ("cognates") and point out the difference in the English and French stress patterns. The student listens to a contrast like English animal vs. French *animal*, academy vs. *académie*, impossibility vs. *impossibilité*, and then attempts the correct French pronunciation. If he carries the English stress pattern into French and pronounces *impossi│bi│lité*, the English and the correct French are contrasted again until he becomes aware of the French pronunciation. Another possible approach, which seems quite profitable in all matters of intonation, is to isolate the French pattern for the student and superimpose it on an English word or sentence—in other words, pronounce English with a French accent: say "impossibility" the way it would be said by a Frenchman. Yet another possibility consists of making the student use the intonation and stress pattern which is used in English when we count: one, two, three, four, et cetera. It so happens that in that particular instance we do pronounce several syllables in succession while giving each syllable the same amount of stress. The student can thus be asked to carry his stress pattern of one-two-three-four over into the pronunciation of French words like: one-two-three, *capital;* one-two-three-four, *animation;* one-two-three-four-five, *amabilité*, and so on.

One of the most important differences between French and English, and from the pedagogical viewpoint one of the most far-reaching, concerns the matter of syllable boundaries. We saw that in English there is at least one stress per word and that in addition there are also two basic types of syllable boundaries: one usually between syllables of the same word, the other between syllables of different words. The result of this kind of stress and juncture pattern is that in English the boundaries between words are fairly well marked off in speech. In French the exact opposite is the case. There are no syllable boundaries which correlate in any helpful manner with the boundaries of words. The exact rules according to which French utterances are divided into syllables are rather complicated, but from the pedagogical point of view it seems useful to remember that (1) the general tendency in French pronunciation is to have open syllables (syllables ending in a vowel), (2) that even if a syllable ends in a consonant, a Frenchman will tend to pronounce this consonant at the beginning of the next syllable rather than at the end of the syllable in which it stands (*pa-rtir*, rather than *par-tir*), (3) that the syllable boundaries have no relation to the word boundaries: *Ils veulent un peu de pain* is thus pronounced somewhat like /i lvœ lœ̃ pø dpɛ̃/.

In English it often happens that the consonants which follow a vowel influence the pronunciation of the preceding vowel, and that glide sounds develop between the vowel and the consonant. Insistence on open syllabification in French will teach the student to avoid the carry-over of this particular speech habit into French. Another point to make in regard to open syllabification is the vowel anticipation of French: in the production of the consonant we must anticipate the lip position required by the following vowel. Thus in saying *pire, tire, qui,* we should spread our lips before we produce the initial consonants in anticipation of the following vowel, just as in the pronunciation of *du, pure, cuve,* we should round our lips before producing the initial consonant in anticipation of the /y/. This is again contrary to English speech habits, where the vowel is influenced by the following consonant rather than the consonant by the following vowel, and strict observation of this mode of articulation will help the student to avoid the wrong glide sounds and diphthongs, which occur in words like *pire* or *pure* if the spreading or rounding of the lips is carried through only after the pronunciation of the consonant, during the pronunciation of the vowel.

We shall only mention the most essential of French intonation patterns, which have been described extensively and with a certain amount of disagreement by various authors. The essential prerequisite for a good French intonation is of course to avoid the English stress pattern with its uneven distribution of emphasis in different syllables and to remember that French is spoken not in words but in syllables which are combined into **stress groups** or **breath groups**. A stress group is a series of syllables (one or several words) which are run together and the last of which receives a slight stress. *C'est impossible!* /sɛ tɛ̃ pɔ sibl/ is one stress group; *Elle ne me l'a pas donné* /ɛl nə mla pa dɔne/, composed of several words, represents only *one* stress group. One might say that from the purely phonetic point of view they are pronounced like one word (they are "phonetic words"). A **breath group** is any sequence of speech that can be pronounced on one breath: it may consist of one or more stress groups. The sentence *ce n'est pas vrai!* is a stress group as well as a breath group. In the sentence *Mon ami qui ne savait pas la réponse était très malheureux*, it is quite possible to pronounce the first part of the utterance up to the end of *réponse* in one breath group, which could most likely be divided into 2 stress groups, one ending with *ami*, the other with *réponse*.

Within each stress group French distinguishes two important basic intonation patterns: one rising and one falling. The rising intonation pattern is typically used in questions which do not begin with interrogative pronouns or adverbs—in other words, questions which can be answered yes or no. The intonation of *Est-elle arrivée hier soir?* may thus be represented by:

Within each group of the type mentioned above, the pitch changes from syllable to syllable rather than within each syllable. Some textbooks prefer, therefore, to represent the intonation pattern above by an arrangement that emphasizes this step-by-step progression in pitch:

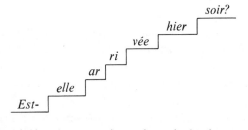

The above description has certain pedagogical advantages, but at the same time it misrepresents the actual modulations of the voice. The intonation thus described is, of course, an overall progression from low to high pitch. But it does not follow the mathematical precision of the pitch intervals of the keyboard on the piano. Nor have linguists been able so far to state with any reasonable agreement or proof that in French there is only a limited number of significant pitch levels. For that reason the general curve diagram is perhaps more advisable or realistic than the "step" arrangement.

The descending type of intonation is often used in questions which begin with an interrogative pronoun or adverb, certain types of exclamation, and commands: *Où sont les livres?*; *Quelle idée!*; *Expliquez-le-lui!*

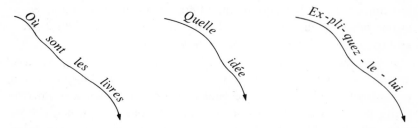

The normal declarative type of sentence is a combination of the two types of intonation patterns described above: a sentence like *J'ai vu mon ami hier soir* could normally be pronounced in two stress groups, one ending with *ami*, the other with *soir*. In the first stress group the rising intonation will be used, in the second the falling. The overall scheme of the sentence may thus be described by using the signs ↗ for rising pitch and ↘ for falling pitch:

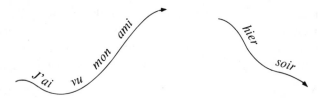

One might say that any declarative statement is the implicit answer to a question: in the first part of the statement our curiosity is aroused by the rising intonation stress group; in the second part (falling pitch) our curiosity is satisfied, and the implicit question is answered at the completion of the statement.

A long declarative statement is usually broken up into a series of ascending groups. Until we get to the "high point" of the statement, each stress or breath group begins on a somewhat higher point than the preceding. After the highest point is reached, each group begins and ends on a somewhat lower point than the preceding one. The sentence is then finished by a group which uses descending intonation. The overall scheme is then somewhat like this:

As for example in:

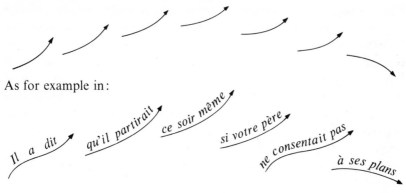

The most frequent mistake made by American students trying to imitate the above type of intonation is to fall back on the same pitch level with each stress group without making any progress in getting to the highest pitch of the sentence. They will produce a monotonous up and down pattern:

Another mistake usually associated with the above is to put heavy stress on the points of high pitch. This is a carry over from the English speech habits in which high pitch and stress are usually correlated.

There are various specific methods of teaching intonation. Pronouncing English sentences with a French intonation is one good way of making the student aware of the French pattern. Another approach is that of contrast within French: we may ask the student to take a series of declarative statements, transform them into questions by the change of intonations only, then transform them into another set of questions by beginning the statements with *pourquoi*, or substituting *qui* for the subject:

1. *Charles est intelligent.*   (⌒↘)
2. *Charles est intelligent?*   (⟋→)
3. *Qui est intelligent?*   (⌒↘)
1. *Robert travaille beaucoup.*   (⟋↘)
2. *Robert travaille beaucoup?* (⟋→)
3. *Qui travaille beaucoup?*   (⌒↘)
1. *Jeanne est fatiguée.*   (⟋↘)
2. *Jeanne est fatiguée?*   (⟋→)
3. *Qui est fatiguée?*   (⌒↘)

The pitch intervals between the syllables of a group depend on the length of the utterance itself. In a short group in which the high point or low point can be reached in a few syllables the intervals can be much larger than in a long group. Many American students have difficulty in judging the correct pitch intervals. In a long utterance they may "run out of pitch" before they have reached the high point. The expansion type of pronunciation exercise is designed to help them with this problem: we start with a sentence like *Il est arrivé*; follow up with additions like *il est arrivé avec lui, il est arrivé avec lui vers trois heures, il est arrivé avec lui vers trois heures de l'après-midi.* This type of exercise not only teaches the student to control the pitch intervals, but also emphasizes the fact that the high pitch point of the sentence (in other words the end of the stress group) may change as the sentence is expanded.

On the elementary level the most important and perhaps the only way to teach French intonation is to insist on correct imitation and on the production of utterances with correct intonation patterns. The teaching of intonation is, therefore, the inevitable and necessary part of any good substitution or transformation exercise or any other type of pattern drill. During the performance of a substitution exercise the pattern, and with it the intonation, stays the same and is learned as part of the drill. In a similar way any transformation exercise (obvious example: ask for the subject or object of a series of sentences, using interrogative pronouns) may involve a shift in intonation pattern. The change of intonation is also an integral part of the transformation performed by the student and is learned as part of the exercise.

(D) ORTHOGRAPHY AND PRONUNCIATION

So far we have been discussing pronunciation problems which a speaker of English would encounter in French even if he were not taught to read and write it. The introduction of French writing presents two new sets of pronunciation problems: one is created by the fact that French writing and speaking do not always correspond; the other arises because the student, already used to giving English phonetic responses to orthographic symbols, may import those responses into French.

French Orthographic Symbols

In French the correspondence between writing and sound is somewhat more predictable than in English. This does not mean that in French the sound-spelling relation is good. Most sounds can be represented by a variety of symbols and at least a few symbols can correspond to different sounds. A brief summary of the French phonemes and their most common possible orthographic equivalents follows:

CONSONANTS

Phoneme	Symbol	Example	Pronunciation
/p/	p	*père*	/pɛʀ/
	pp	*appartement*	/apaʀtəmã/
	b	*obtient*	/ɔptjɛ̃/
/t/	t	*ton*	/tɔ̃/
	tt	*attendre*	/atãdʀ/
	d	*grand homme*	/gʀãtɔm/
/k/	c	*car*	/kaʀ/
	k	*kilo*	/kilo/
	q	*cinq*	/sɛ̃k/
	ch	*chrétien*	/kʀetjɛ̃/
	qu	*quand*	/kã/
	x	*excuse*	/ɛkskyz/
/b/	b	*beau*	/bo/
	bb	*abbé*	/abe/
/d/	d	*donner*	/dɔne/
	dd	*addition*	/adisjɔ̃/
/g/	g	*gant*	/gã/
	gu	*guerre*	/gɛʀ/
	c	*second*	/sgɔ̃/
	x	*examen*	/ɛgzamɛ̃/
/f/	f	*faim*	/fɛ̃/
	ff	*siffler*	/sifle/
	ph	*téléphone*	/telefɔn/
/s/	s	*sentir*	/sãtiʀ/
	ss	*assez*	/ase/
	c	*cent*	/sã/
	ç	*français*	/fʀãsɛ/
	t	*attention*	/atãsjɔ̃/
	x	*dix*	/dis/
	sc	*scie*	/si/

Phoneme	Symbol	Example	Pronunciation
/ʃ/	ch	*cher*	/ʃɛʀ/
	sch	*schéma*	/ʃema/
/ʒ/	j	*jeu*	/ʒø/
	g	*général*	/ʒeneʀal/
	ge	*mangeais*	/mãʒɛ/
/v/	v	*vingt*	/vɛ̃/
	f	*neuf ans*	/nœvã/
	w	*wagon*	/vɑgɔ̃/
/z/	s	*rose*	/ʀoz/
	x	*deuxième*	/døzjɛm/
	z	*zero*	/zeʀo/
/l/	l	*alors*	/alɔʀ/
	ll	*aller*	/ale/
/ʀ/	r	*rat*	/ʀa/
	rr	*errer*	/ɛʀe/
	rh	*rhume*	/ʀym/
/m/	m	*main*	/mɛ̃/
	mm	*commencer*	/kɔmãse/
/n/	n	*non*	/nɔ̃/
	nn	*donner*	/dɔne/
	mn	*automne*	/otɔn/
/ɲ/	gn	*agneau*	/aɲo/

SEMIVOWELS

Phoneme	Symbol	Example	Pronunciation
/j/	i	*vient*	/vjɛ̃/
	il	*travail*	/tʀavaj/
	lle	*fille*	/fij/
	ille	*maille*	/maj/
	i, ï	*païen*	/pajɛ̃/
	y	*yeux*	/jø/
/w/	ou (+ i)	*Louis*	/lwi/
	o (+ i)	*loi*	/lwa/
/ɥ/	u (+ i)	*lui*	/lɥi/

Vowels

Phoneme	Symbol	Example	Pronunciation
/i/	i	lit	/li/
	î	île	/il/
	y	style	/stil/
/e/	e	essai	/esɛ/
	é	parlé	/paʀle/
	er	parler	/paʀle/
	ez	parlez	/paʀle/
	ai	parlai	/paʀle/
	ei	neiger	/neʒe/
/ɛ/	e	bette	/bɛt/
	è	élève	/elɛv/
	ê	bête	/bɛt/
	ë	Noël	/nɔɛl/
	ei	neige	/nɛʒ/
	ai	aime	/ɛm/
	aî	maître	/mɛtʀ/
	é	événement	/evɛnmã/
/a/	a	parle	/paʀl/
	à	à	/a/
	e	femme	/fam/
	oi	moi	/mwa/
	oy	voyons	/vwajɔ̃/
	oe	moelle	/mwal/
/ɑ/	â	âme	/ɑm/
	a	classe	/klɑs/
	oi	trois	/tʀwɑ/
	oê	poêle	/pwɑl/
/ɔ/	o	botte	/bɔt/
	au	Paul	/pɔl/
	ô	hôpital	/ɔpital/
/o/	o	dos	/do/
	ô	tôt	/to/
	au	fausse	/fos/
	eau	beau	/bo/

Phoneme	Symbol	Example	Pronunciation
/u/	ou	*doux*	/du/
	oû	*coûte*	/kut/
/y/	u (û)	*sur, sûr*	/syʀ/
	eu	*eu*	/y/
/ø/	eu	*feu*	/fø/
	oeu	*oeufs*	/ø/
/œ/	eu	*leur*	/lœʀ/
	oeu	*oeuf*	/œf/
	oe	*oeil*	/œj/
	ue	*cueille*	/kœj/
/ə/	e	*leçon*	/ləsɔ̃/
	ai	*nous faisons*	/nufəzɔ̃/
	on	*monsieur*	/məsjø/
/œ̃/	un	*un*	/œ̃/
	um	*humble*	/œ̃bl/
/ɛ̃/	im	*impossible*	/ɛ̃pɔsibl/
	in	*vin*	/vɛ̃/
	ain	*vain*	/vɛ̃/
	aim	*faim*	/fɛ̃/
	ein	*sein*	/sɛ̃/
	eim	*Reims*	/ʀɛ̃s/
	en	*vient*	/vjɛ̃/
	yn	*synchronique*	/sɛ̃kʀɔnik/
	ym	*symphonie*	/sɛ̃fɔni/
ɔ̃/	om	*comprendre*	/kɔ̃pʀãdʀ/
	on	*dont*	/dɔ̃/
/ã/	an	*an*	/ã/
	am	*chambre*	/ʃãbʀ/
	en	*en*	/ã/
	em	*ensemble*	/ãsãbl/

The types of possible mistakes which arise from the lack of correspondence between sound and symbol in French are, of course, quite familiar to the French teacher. Let us review some of the most common: (1) /ã/ instead of /ɛ̃/ in words like *bien*, *vient*; (2) /ɛ̃/ instead of

/ã/ in *cent*, *en*; (3) /d/ instead of /t/ in *grand homme*, *médecin*; (4) /ɛl/ instead of /aj/ in *travail*, because the student interprets *-ail* as *ai + l* rather than *a + il*; (5) /l/ rather than /j/ in *fille*, perhaps under the influence of *ville*, *tranquille*, in which *ille* is pronounced /il/; (6) /ɛ/ or /ẽ/ instead of /a/ in *femme*; (7) /ɔ/ in *monsieur* because of spelling *mon* (= mɔ̃). A second source of mistakes is the interference of English orthography. Some of the most typical follow: (1) /n/ or /m/ fully pronounced after nasal vowels like *monter* or *tomber*; (2) the pronunciation [ʃən] for the ending *-tion*, instead of /sjɔ̃/; (3) the reflex [tʃ] instead of /ʃ/ for *ch* as in *cheval*; (4) the pronunciation [dʒ] instead of /ʒ/ as in *rage*, *général*; (5) pronunciations like /oij/ or /oi/ for *oi*; (6) *il* pronounced /il/ in words like *travail*; (7) *qu* pronounced /kw/ instead of /k/; (8) pronunciation /h/ for a silent *h* or aspirated *h* (the latter indicating in French the absence of linking (see below) rather than any sound); (9) the pronunciation of the various silent consonant symbols of the noun or verb endings.

The Mute e; Liaison; Linking

The lack of correspondence between French speech and orthography in connection with the "mute" or "fleeting" *e*, and the liaison and linking habits cause very special types of problems, basically connected with the tendency of French toward open syllabification.

The /ə/ is often called "fleeting" because it may or may not be pronounced, according to varying circumstances. The complete set of rules indicating when an *e* should be pronounced /ə/ and when it should be silent is rather complicated. We shall only summarize the essential rules. The overall principle governing the use of the /ə/ sound is the "law of three consonants." Since French people try to speak in open syllables, they attempt to pronounce the last consonant of a syllable as if it belonged to the beginning of the next. This can occur only if the next syllable begins (1) in a vowel, (2) in one consonant, or (3) a consonant cluster capable of beginning an utterance. The corollary of this is that French speakers as a rule will avoid pronouncing together most (though not necessarily all) combinations of three consonants.

The most important rules for the dropping of *e* are the following:

1. Within a phrase or word the /ə/ is dropped after one pronounced consonant and retained after two. If we indicate dropping of /ə/ by

ȩ, retaining by *e*, then: *tu lȩ sais; mon pȩtit; pas dȩ lait; parfaitȩment.* But: *elle le sait; appartement; quatre sous; parle-moi.*

2. If two or more /ə/ sounds follow each other in successive syllables and are separated by only one consonant, then every other /ə/ can be dropped (if one /ə/ is dropped, two consonants will come together). This means that the next /ə/ must be pronounced: *je lȩ trouve: je nȩ le dȩmande pas: je nȩ me lȩ redȩmande pas*, et cetera.

3. /ə/ is generally dropped whenever it is preceded by a single pronounced consonant: *trop de pain* /tʀodpɛ̃/.

There are some exceptions to the above rules. The most important are the following:

1. In the group *je ne*, the first *e* must be pronounced: *je nȩ sais pas: je nȩ dis pas cela.*

2. The pronoun *le*, if it follows the verb (imperative), must be fully pronounced: *fais-le! dis-le!*

3. The /ə/ which is followed by an "h-aspiré" must be pronounced: *le héros; une harpe.*

4. /ə/ must be pronounced before *ri* + *vowel*, in order to avoid the combination *consonant* + *rj: seriez, donnerions, feriez.*

The usually silent (orthographically) final consonant of a word is often pronounced if it is followed (within the same stress group) by a word that begins with a vowel (or also orthographically with a "mute h"). This process of pronouncing the final consonant is called **liaison.** We normally say /nu/ (nous) but *nous allons* /nuzalɔ̃/. The following vowel of *allons* allows us to pronounce the final *s* of *nous* as if it were the initial consonant of the following syllable.

Again the complete set of rules governing *liaison* is quite complex. Many *liaisons* are made or omitted according to style and utterance: colloquial French observes fewer liaisons than more formal speech. The optional types of liaison (**liaisons facultatives**) vary greatly according to the individual as well as according to style and occasion. Some of them are made very frequently, as for instance the liaison between the impersonal third person of *être* and the following adjective (*C'était impossible*); others are extremely rare, for instance the liaison between plural noun or adjective and the following verb (*Mes amis arrivent*). We shall be content to summarize the most important types of *liaisons* which must be made (**liaisons obligatoires**), and the most important of those which should not be made under any circumstances (**liaisons interdites**).

Liaisons Obligatoires

1. The article or any word that can replace the article (the *determinative*—see morphology) are in liaison with the following noun or adjective: (Article + noun, adjective):

les‿enfants   les‿autres‿amis
mon‿enfant
mes‿enfants   mes‿autres‿enfants
deux‿enfants   mes‿autres‿élèves
quels‿enfants   vos‿autres‿idées
leurs‿enfants

2. Adjective + noun:

petit‿enfant
petits‿enfants

3. Pronoun + verb, or verb + pronoun:

vous‿êtes
nous‿arrivons
allez‿-y
ont‿-ils

4. Pronoun + pronoun-adverb + verb, or verb + pronoun + pronoun (pronoun + adverb):

vous‿y êtes
nous les‿y mettons
allons-nous‿-en
mettez-les‿-y

5. Monosyllabic preposition + (anything) or monosyllabic adverb + (anything):

dans‿un hôtel   très‿important
sous‿un arbre   pas‿important
sans‿argent   moins‿agréable

Liaisons Interdites

1. Singular noun/ + (anything) or any proper name/ + (anything):

un soldat / anglais   Louis / est intelligent
un plan / important   Paris / est la capitale
un projet / intéressant   Jean / est arrivé

2. *Et/* + anything:

> *Jean et | Anne*
> *Lui et | elle*

3. Anything/ + "*h-aspiré*" + anything:

> *en | hongrois*
> *les | haricots verts*
> *les | hautes montagnes*

4. Interrogative adverb + (anything):

> *quand | est-il arrivé?*
> *comment | a-t-il appris cela?*

The exceptions to the above rules occur rarely and only in some fixed expressions, such as: *comment allez-vous?* /kɔmãtalevu/ in spite of the rule (4), or *pot au feu* /potofø/ in spite of rule (1) concerning the *liaisons interdites*.

A special word concerning the liaison of *n*: the general principle of French pronunciation with regard to the nasal consonant is that the nasal consonant is not pronounced after a nasal vowel and that in turn the vowel preceding it becomes nasalized: conversely, a vowel followed by a pronounced nasal consonant is usually not nasalized. Thus we pronounce a vowel + n, or a vowel + n + consonant as a nasal vowel, as in *don* /dɔ̃/, *dont* /dɔ̃/, *tenter* /tãte/, but a vowel + m(n) + vowel as an oral vowel followed by /n/ or /m/, as in *Anne* /an/, or *Jeanne* /ʒan/. If in the liaison a final -*n* becomes pronounced, the normal result is that the preceding vowel denasalizes: *ancien* /ãsjɛ̃/ but *ancien ami* /ãsjɛnami/; *plein* /plɛ̃/ but *plein air* /plɛnɛʀ/; *bon* /bɔ̃/ but *bon ami* /bɔnami/. There are only a few words in which the final -*n* becomes pronounced in liaison and the preceding vowel retains its nasal quality. They are *un, on, en, bien, rien,* and with some Frenchmen, also *mon, ton, son, bon.* Thus we say *on a parle* /ɔ̃naparle/; *un autre enfant* /œ̃notʀãfã/; *en ete* /ã nete/. These single syllable words in liaison are today the only fossil remnants of an early stage of French during which nasal vowels were normally followed by nasal consonants.

Even the simplified general rules for the use of the "fleeting *e*" and the liaison of final consonants that we have given here are after all fairly complicated. They represent the minimum that the teacher or advanced student ought to know. Obviously the student in his first and perhaps second year of French could not handle these rules. The use or nonuse of the /ə/ or of liaison must ultimately be acquired as a matter of imitation and habit, and cannot possibly be controlled with a set of rules governing the pronunciation of orthographic symbols. Approached from the viewpoint of speech alone, all of the important cases of liaison and /ə/ involve, basically, the use of alternate grammatical forms in specific position. Thus, liaison and /ə/ are really part of the grammar of spoken French rather than a matter of pronunciation. The best way of teaching liaison and /ə/ is, therefore, to present them as part of the grammar (especially morphology) of the French language.

Perhaps the most serious lack of correspondence between French orthography and pronunciation is due to the so-called linking habits, which we have already alluded to in our discussion of syllabification. *Linking* is just another way of saying that French is spoken in syllables rather than in words. The syllable boundaries of speech have no necessary relation to the word boundaries, the boundaries between the semantic units which appear on the printed or written page.

The native speaker of English is used to having most word boundaries clearly expressed in his speech. In addition, he is apt to learn French by remembering words. If he has read a French sentence he retains a visual memory of how this sentence is divided into words. All this leads him to expect to find some sort of word boundaries when he hears a French sentence. Since the French utterance does not contain any clues as to where the word boundaries are, the student has a major comprehension problem. In writing, the semantic divisions of an utterance are marked by neat spaces between words: what the student sees is: *notre petit Robert est arrivé ce matin.* The phonetic transcription of what he hears is: /nɔ tRə pti Rɔ bɛ Rɛ ta Ri ve sma tɛ̃/. The result of this lack of correspondence between orthographic representation and speech is, of course, that a student often will not recognize the spoken form of a sentence even though he may be perfectly familiar with its written form.

The lack of exact correspondence between French sounds and symbols, the problem of the mute *e* and liaison, the lack of word boundaries in speech, the possible interference coming from English orthography, all add up to some rather formidable reasons why speaking and comprehension in the initial stages of learning should be completely disassociated from reading and writing. Reading and writing reinforce speaking and listening only after a particular amount of material has been mastered in speaking and understanding. In the initial stages of learning they interfere with each other and pull the learner's attention in opposite directions. The *dictée* for instance, one of the most frequently used teaching and learning devices in the French class, is as such not a method to teach aural comprehension. It is primarily a test to find out (1) whether the student does comprehend French, (2) whether he is mastering French grammar and its orthography. If the student does not understand spoken French to begin with, the *dictée* is not going to teach him to understand it. Of course, it is true that the *dictée*, if used frequently in the course, will contribute to the improvement of the aural comprehension of the student. But this will happen because the student is forced to listen to French, and not because he is forced to write down what he is hearing. The writing as such serves only one teaching purpose, a rather important one to be sure: to give the student some practice in the use of French orthography.

Because of the lack of absolute correspondence between French orthography and pronunciation, some teachers and textbooks make use of either phonetic or phonemic transcription (in a phonetic transcription features which are not phonemically significant such as vowel length are included, whereas a strictly phonemic transcription uses the same symbol for all the different allophones of the same phoneme). There are different ways of using a phonemic transcription. It may be used throughout the course for the purpose of classifying problems of grammar and pronunciation; it may be used throughout as the regular accompaniment of the presentation of French orthography; it may also be used in the initial stages of the course only, with the switch to regular French orthography being made as soon as the student has developed good pronunciation habits. The obvious advantage of the phonemic transcription is that it establishes a one-to-one correspondence between sound and symbol. The obvious disadvantage is that unless we are interested in teaching only speaking and aural comprehension, the orthography must be taught sooner or later, and the student exposed to two writing systems may be more confused than ever. Another objection that can be raised against the use of phonetic or phonemic transcription is that it is of comparatively little use in the teaching of at least two speech-writing conflicts: (1) The clash between semantic units and speech. A transcription like /nu za vɔ̃ de za mi/ will make this particular problem clear to the student but it does not really solve it; (2) The symbols used in phonetic transcription such as /e/, /ʀ/, /t/, /a/, are so close to English orthographic symbols that they may still invite English rather than French responses.

(E) SUMMARY OF PROBLEMS AND METHODS

In concluding our discussion of the teaching of French pronunciation we shall summarize very briefly the chief problems encountered by the student. This list can serve as a sort of check list that a French teacher may use to evaluate a student's pronunciation or a guide to be kept in mind in correcting pronunciation mistakes:

1. Mispronunciation of the rounded front vowels /y/ (*rue*), /ø/ (*feu*), /œ/ (*peur*).

2. Mispronunciation of the nasals by putting an /n/ after them: pronouncing *dans* as /dãn/ instead of /dã/.

3. Diphthongization of the French vowels /i/, /e/, /o/, /u/—"see" instead of *si*, "lay" instead of *les*, "bow" instead of *beau*, and "do" instead of *doux*.

4. Aspiration of the initial voiceless stops.

5. Pronunciation of alveolar /t/ and /d/.

6. Pronunciation of an English /r/ or /l/.

7. Failure to pronounce fully and explode the final consonants in words like *patte* /pat/, *digue* /dig/.

8. Use of English stress patterns in French words, for instance, pronouncing *liberté* with stress on the initial syllable.

9. Making marked pauses (English open juncture) between French words.

10. Avoiding the running together of words and open syllabification in favor of the English syllable pattern.

If the student has learned French orthography, then the teacher must see to it that he does not:

1. Miss the obvious cases of liaison as in *les amis*.

2. Pronounce /ə/ which no Frenchman would pronounce in normal conversation, as in *promenade*.

3. Give obvious spelling pronunciations.

4. React to French orthographic symbols as if they were English.

The teaching methods which we have discussed may be summarized as follows:

1. Insist on correct or at least increasingly correct imitation in choral and individual response exercise.

2. Develop auditory discrimination between French phonemes through special exercises such as the contrasting of minimal pairs.

3. Develop auditory discrimination between English and French sounds.

4. Describe the correct French articulation to the student.

5. Use diagrams to indicate intonation patterns.

6. Use gradually expanded sentences to teach intonation.

Some other methods of teaching pronunciation usually employed in special courses but which can also be employed at the elementary level are:

1. The use of diagrams showing the positions of the speech organs during the production of specific difficult sounds.

2. The use of exercises in which difficult sounds are repeated in specially devised phrases (such as *ton thé t'a-t-il ôté ta toux?*).

3. The use of either phonetic or phonemic transcription.

In conclusion, we can only reiterate that the teaching of French pronunciation cannot be dissociated from the teaching of grammatical patterns; that the acquisition of a good pronunciation depends very largely on the possibility of having in the initial stages of the French course a period in which French orthography is not used at all and during which first aural discrimination and then correct pronunciation can be established. The optimal length of the prereading period is uncertain. It varies, no doubt, according to the type of course, the age and aptitudes of the learner; but perhaps even more essential than the prereading period is the principle already alluded to above, that in the first stage of instruction (perhaps the first two years of high school) audio-lingual contact with all new material should precede reading and writing.

CHAPTER VII

Teaching Morphology

(A) GENERAL CONCEPTS

The smallest units of speech, the phonemes, have the power to differentiate meaning; but they themselves are meaningless. They are, however, combined into larger units, larger building stones which have recognizable meanings: the larger units are called **morphemes**. Morphemes are then the smallest units of speech which have an identifiable meaning of their own. Linguists identify morphemes in about the same way in which they isolate phonemes, namely by comparing utterances and observing the identical and different elements. Thus if we compare *allons* /alɔ̃/ with *allez* /ale/, we can readily see that *all-* /al-/ is common to both of them; it is, therefore, an independent building stone that can be used again in other phrases like *nous allions* /nuzal jɔ̃/, *il alla* /il ala/, et cetera. If we compare *allons!* /alɔ̃/ with *parlons!* /paʀlɔ̃/ we see that *-ons* /ɔ̃/ is also a building stone that can be taken out of the utterance and be used in another verb form. The comparison of *allez!* /ale/ with *parlez!* /paʀle/ teaches us the same thing about the ending *-ez* /e/. Thus *all-* /al/, *-ons* /ɔ̃/, *-ez* /e/ are all morphemes of the French language.

Morphemes are not necessarily identical with syllables or words: *allons* is one word but two morphemes, whereas *vais* is one word and one morpheme. If we inspect a word like *fatigue*, we find that it has two syllables but neither of the two, *fa* or *tigue* represents a building stone that appears anywhere else in the same recognizable meaning that it has in *fatigue*. Thus the two syllables of *fatigue* are only one morpheme.

In the discussion of the phoneme we found that the very same phoneme can appear in different forms according to the environment, thus having **allophones**. A similar statement can also be made about morphemes. The very same building stone can appear in different forms according to its environment, and the same morpheme can have different allomorphs. For instance, the utterance books is composed of two morphemes: book, and -s/s/ indicating plural. If we inspect the utterance dishes, we find it is composed of dish and -es /ɪz/. Taking a look at hands, we see that it is composed of hand and the plural indicator -s, now pronounced /z/. Now /s/, /ɪz/, /z/ have all the same meaning, "plural," and the occurrence of such variants is predictable: /s/ appears only after unvoiced consonants, /z/ appears only after vowels and voiced consonants, and /ɪz/ only after sibilants. All these three sounds are allomorphs of the same building stone or morpheme.

The teaching application of morphemic analysis lies principally in two directions. The methods used in the isolation of morphemes—inspection for similar and different elements—can be converted into teaching methods in the presentation of the morphology of French. Compare *ils disent la vérité* /ildizla veʀite/, *ils regardent le livre* /il ʀəgaʀd lə livʀ/, with *nous disons la vérité* /nu dizɔ̃ la veʀite/, *nous regardons le livre* /nu ʀəgaʀdɔ̃ lə livr/. We find that in speech the first two of the sentences are different from the second two in the following ways: /il/ is replaced by /nu/ and the ending /ɔ̃/ appears in the second pair of sentences only. This allows the linguist to isolate /il/, /nu/ and /ɔ̃/ and identify them as morphemes of French. The importance of this for teaching lies not in this discovery but in the method employed; for a pattern exercise in which the student shifts the first series of sentences into the second by changing *ils* to *nous*, while adding *-ons* to the verb stem, teaches the student the use of these building stones in the French language.

The other contribution of morphemic analysis to French teaching lies also in the application of a point of view rather than in a general discovery: the analysis of the linguist is, of course, applied to the spoken language rather than to its written form. In the case of a language like French in which the oral form is so very different from its orthographic representation, linguistic analysis leads to a description of the language that is quite different from the one found in most of the conventional grammars, based primarily on the written form of French. To give a few examples: in oral French many morphemes, especially those signaling grammatical meaning, have different forms, usually depending on whether they stand before a consonant or a vowel. We say *les livres* /le livʀ/, but *les enfants* /lez ɑ̃fɑ̃/. Some morphemes have three different forms depending on whether they stand before a vowel a consonant, or a pause: *dix* /di/ *livres*; *dix* /diz/ *enfants*; *il y en a dix* /dis/. These *allomorphs* are not differently represented in orthography. In turn there are forms which are different in French orthography, but pronounced alike: *il parle, ils parlent*. The usual approach to these differences between spoken and written French is to explain them in terms of pronunciation. Rules concerning *liaison* or statements like "the third person ending *-ent* is silent" are thus in fact recipes telling us how to read French aloud, rather than how to speak it. They assume that the student, whenever he speaks French, is, in fact, reading French either from a real or an imaginary printed page.

There is no question that interposing orthography between the speaker and the oral language in this way slows down the student's ability in comprehension as well as in speaking. In a course in which we teach only speaking and understanding, or in the organization of the **prereading instruction period** of any course (for example, the first two or three years of French in the elementary schools or the first semester in High School), grammar based entirely on the written language would be unusable. But even if oral and written French are presented concurrently or almost concurrently, it is better to point out to the student what he is actually hearing and saying rather than to use the orthographic picture as the basis of his learning. To give an example: the student should first be put through exercises which make it clear that the plural article has two forms, /le/ as in *les livres*, and /lez/ as in *les enfants*. After the student has listened to these two articles, and learned to use them, he can be told that we use the same orthographic representation *les* for both of them. The student who fails to pronounce the /z/ in /lezɑ̃fɑ̃/ is, in fact, not merely mispronouncing, he is using a wrong grammatical form, a wrong allomorph. His mistake is comparable to the one a learner of English might make in giving the plural of dish as dishs rather than dishes, or saying a apple instead of an apple.

In our discussion we shall not attempt to present a complete analysis of all French morphology, but we shall try to examine those morphemic patterns which signal the main grammatical relationships and we shall try to present those patterns as they appear in oral French to the student who is trying to learn to speak and understand the language without the interference of orthographic representation.

In our presentation of morphology we shall not introduce extensively new linguistic terminology or categories. The nomenclature applied to word classes and endings is in itself relatively unimportant. And since most students and teachers have some familiarity with traditional nomenclature such as verb, noun, adjective, substantive, there seems little justification for coining new terms. New nomenclature seems justified only when the traditional nomenclature is downright misleading or when the new terminology makes a positive contribution to the student's understanding of the grammatical pattern. To give examples: "Present Subjunctive" is probably a bad name for a tense which can refer to an action in the Present, Future, and—in colloquial French at least—in the Past: *J'ai peur qu'il ne vienne demain* (I am afraid he'll come tomorrow); *J'avais peur qu'il ne vienne* (I was afraid he was coming). A term like **Timeless Subjunctive** (suggested by Prof. R. A. Hall), or just **Subjunctive No. 1,** or **Normal Subjunctive** might be more appropriate. To call the tense of *J'ai donné* a "Past Indefinite" (*Passé Indéfini*) is not a very good idea: the purely descriptive term "Compound Past" (**Passé Composé**) is certainly preferable. The Passé Composé has indeed the function of a Past Indefinite: it is used to denote a past action if the exact time of performance is irrelevant to the speaker: *J'ai été à Paris* (I have been in Paris), but in spoken French it has also taken over the function of a Past Definite: *Hier j'ai vu Charles* (Yesterday I saw Charles). The result is that the name Past Indefinite actually interferes with the student's understanding of the meaning and function of the tense. To call *mon* or *ce* "possessive" or "demonstrative" adjectives has also certain disadvantages. True, they modify nouns, but at the same time they differ quite sharply from adjectives: they can be used instead, but never with the article (*mon grand livre, le grand livre*). Unlike the adjective, they do not form adverbs, and they can never be used as predicates after the verb *être* (*Le livre est grand*). For this reason it seems preferable not to talk about possessive or demonstrative adjectives. A classification which groups *mon, ce* with all the other words which in a syntactical pattern are alternatives of the article, and designates them as **noun determinors** or **determinatives** makes a grammatical point missed by the conventional nomenclature.

Some linguists have attempted to introduce new nomenclature in order to make it clear that their classifications are not based on the same criteria as those that are used to establish the traditional categories.

According to the traditional point of view, semantic criteria are used to establish word classes: thus nouns are classified as names for persons and things; verbs denote actions, and so forth. Two objections can be made to this type of classification. First of all, it is vague. As a recent linguistic's book points out, a "home run" is neither a person nor a thing; it is probably an action, even though we all agree that home run is a noun and not a verb.

The second objection—perhaps more important from the pedagogical point of view—is that the classification according to semantic criteria assumes somehow that we are dealing with a language that we already know. A linguist who is interested in writing the grammar of a language with which he is not yet familiar (a rather typical situation for the anthropological linguist) cannot ask his native informant how verbs are expressed in his language. He must find this out for himself. For this reason he is, initially at least, not much interested in the fact that some words express actions and other qualities or things. He must find out why certain words can be grouped into the same class. He must establish the purely formal characteristics that enable certain groups of words to express similar concepts and have similar functions. In the sentence The father beats the child, we know of course, that father and child are nouns and beats is the verb, but what interests the linguist primarily is how and why we know this. Thus we know that father and child are nouns because they are preceded by the, and we know that beat is a verb because it stands between the two nouns and because it takes an -s in the third person singular. Linguists classify words, therefore, according to formal criteria. Words belong to the same class because they can take the same ending or because they can be substituted for each other in the same syntactical patterns. Now the point of view of the student studying a foreign language is basically similar to that of the linguist analyzing a new language. To find out that nouns are the names of persons, things, places, is no help in speaking or understanding the language. What the student must learn are the formal features that enable him to recognize and to use word classes. To define nouns as those words which must follow a noun determinor (*mon, son, ce, le*) may seem a rather strange and circular way of getting at a concept, but the pedagogical application of the procedure is quite clear: the student can be trained to recognize in written form, and especially in speech, the **noun determinors** as clues for the following noun, and this in turn will enable him to get a clearer understanding and auditory comprehension of the French construction.

(B) THE NOUN AND THE DETERMINATIVE

In oral French the majority of French nouns are invariable in both singular and plural, since the final -*s* which expresses the plural in orthography has normally no equivalent in speech. The *liaison* at the end of a plural noun is optional and usually not observed in colloquial French: *les filles arrivent* /lefijzaRiv/ is quite rare. There are of course a few nouns which have special plural forms: they are the nouns which have *irregular plurals; canal/canaux, cheval/chevaux* (but *bal/bals, festival/festivals*), *travail/travaux, vantail/vantaux* (but *détail/détails*), *ciel/cieux, oeil/yeux, aieul/aieux, oeuf/oeufs* /œf/: /ø/ and *boeuf/boeufs* /bœf/: /bø/. A spoken -*s* as a plural marker is very rare: it exists only in the noun *les moeurs* /lemœRs/, and in the pronoun *tous*.

Whether a noun in French is singular or plural is generally expressed orally not by the noun itself but by the word preceding the noun: *le livre* /lə livR/, *mon livre* /mɔ̃ livR/, *ce livre* /sə livR/, are singular while *les livres* /le livR/, *mes livres* /me livR/, *ces livres* /se livR/, are plural. In English the differences between singular and plural is expressed by the ending of the noun itself (/-s/, /-z/, /-ɪz/). This means that in the matter of recognizing number both English speech and French orthography conspire to divert the attention of the student away from the place where it should be (the word or words preceding the noun) to where it should not be (the end of the noun itself).

The singular/plural difference is thus usually expressed by the words which we referred to as the **determinatives**. As we have pointed out, these words share certain characteristics: (1) They are mutually exclusive: a noun cannot be modified by more than one determinative; (2) they can occur only as modifiers of nouns. In our discussion of syntax we shall refer to them as **noun satellites**.

The determinatives may be classed in several groups according to whether they express the singular/plural and masculine/feminine contrasts.

The first group includes the **definite article** (and the contractions of the article with *à* and *de*), the **possessive determinatives** of singular possessors (*mon, ton, son*) and the demonstrative determinative (*ce*). These determinatives can always express the difference between singular and plural, and they also express the difference between masculine and feminine in the singular, except before words beginning with a vowel. The following table may serve to summarize these facts:

SINGULAR					PLURAL			
Masculine		*Feminine*	*Before a Vowel*		Masculine / Feminine		*Before a Vowel*	
le	/lə/	*la* /la/	*l'*	/l/	*les*	/le/	*les*	/lez/
du	/dy/	*de la* /dəla/	*de l'*	/dəl/	*des*	/de/	*des*	/dez/
au	/o/	*à la* (a la)	*à l'*	/al/	*aux*	/o/	*aux*	/oz/
mon	/mɔ̃/	*ma* (ma)	*mon*	/mɔ̃n/	*mes*	/me/	*mes*	/mez/
ton	/tɔ̃/	*ta* /ta/	*ton*	/tɔ̃n/	*tes*	/te/	*tes*	/tez/
son	/sɔ̃/	*sa* /sa/	*son*	/sɔ̃n/	*ses*	/se/	*ses*	/sez/
ce	/sə/	*cette* /sɛt/	*cet*, m. *cette*, f.	/sɛt/	*ces*	/se/	*ces*	/sez/

The above table shows quite clearly that the only masculine/feminine contrast before a vowel is the purely **orthographic** distinction between *cet* (*cet enfant*) and *cette* (*cette échelle*). Some Frenchmen also try to preserve a masculine/feminine distinction before vowels with *mon, ton, son* by nasalizing the /ɔ/ of the masculine form (*mon ami* = mɔ̃nami) and denasalizing the /ɔ/ of the feminine (*mon amie* = mɔnami). A rather special problem is also created by the words beginning with the *h-aspiré*. Since this *h* is in modern French just as silent as the *h* of *homme* or *honneur*, the *h-aspiré* words can, from the point of view of oral French, be presented best as words which, although they begin with a vowel, are treated as if they begin with a consonant; such as *le héros*, or *ma hache*. The final /ə/ of a form like *cette* /sɛtə/ is also pronounced before these words: *cette hache* /sɛtəaʃ/. The most important pedagogical application of the above analysis is simply that the prevocalic forms should be taught and drilled as distinct forms independent of the masculine/feminine contrast. Thus in exercises involving shifting from singular to plural (*voici l'enfant/voici les enfants, voici l'échelle/voici les échelles*) the student should be made aware of the fact that the singular/plural difference is expressed by an alternation /l/ : /lez/. The same principle should be pointed out in the alternations /mɔ̃n/ : /mez/, /al/ : /oz/, /sɛt/ : /sez/. In substitution exercises the student must be drilled to repeat and then to produce by choice the correct determinative required by the substitution word: *voici les* /le/ *livres* . . . substitute *enfants* . . . *voici les* /lez/ *enfants*, et cetera. Thus the correct speech habits must be established as a matter of the choice of a grammatical form rather than as a rule governing the pronunciation of *les* before vowels. Mistakes like *ce homme* or *ma ami* can be avoided quite easily if the student is drilled from the very beginning in the fact that only one form is possible before a vowel. The student must be drilled to use /mɔ̃n/, /tɔ̃n/, /sɔ̃n/, /sɛt/ quite automatically in a pattern like *Voici mon livre, Où est ce cahier* whenever the suggested substitution noun begins with a vowel.

We can consider *votre* and *notre* a separate group of determinatives, since unlike *mon, ton, son,* they never express the masculine/feminine contrast. They always express the singular/plural difference: *notre/nos, votre/vos.* Again, the plural forms before vowels (/noz/ and /voz/ as in *nos amis* /nozami/ and *vos amis* /vozami/) should be drilled as distinct speech forms. The student should also become aware of the pronunciation /nɔt/ and /vɔt/ for *notre* and *votre* which are quite current in normal colloquial speech. The full pronunciation of the *tr* cluster does in many cases require the pronunciation of the final /ə/ in order to avoid clusters of three consonants: *notre père* /nɔtRə pɛR/. Again the form with the final /ə/ is required also before the *h-aspiré* words: *notre héros* /nɔtRəeRo/.

The determinatives *leur* and *quel* express the singular/plural difference only before vowels: *leur* /lœR/ *enfant; leurs* /lœRz/ *enfants: quel* /kɛl/ *enfant; quels* /kɛlz/ *enfants,* but *leur livres; leurs livres* or *quelle femme; quelles femmes* sound, of course, exactly alike. Again the *h-aspiré* words furnish us with an exception: not only do they act like words beginning with a consonant (*quel héros* sounds of course like *quels héros*), but since the /ə/ is always pronounced before these words they can indicate a masculine/feminine distinction in the singular: *quel héros* /kɛl eRo/ but *quelle hache* /kɛlə aʃ/.

The indefinite article *un* is in a class by itself insofar as it is the only noun determinative which always expresses the difference between masculine and feminine, even before vowels: *un* /œ̃/ *livre, une* /yn/ *femme, une* /yn/ *échelle, un* /œ̃n/ *ami, une* /ynə/ *hache.* The indefinite article has thus four forms in spoken French: two masculine ones: /œ̃/ and /œ̃n/, two feminine ones: /yn/ and /ynə/. Since it always expresses the masculine/feminine contrast it is the logical form with which to introduce new nouns and also the logical base form with which to start transformation exercises involving the use of the other determinatives. For instance, a student may be asked to substitute different nouns (they could be the names of objects actually presented by the teacher) in a pattern like: *Voici un livre. Quel livre est-ce? C'est mon livre. C'est le livre de votre professeur.*

In summary, then, the teaching of the morphology of the determinative can take the form of substitution and transformation exercises in which the student is forced to choose forms required by the shift from singular to plural or from one person to the next, or by the substitution of different nouns. Since the plural/singular contrast is often not grasped by the student, it also seems advisable to give the student comprehension exercises in which he simply indicates whether the nouns in the sentences are in the singular or plural, or whether a singular/plural difference was expressed at all, for instance, *Voici les enfants* (student answers: plural), *Voici leurs enfants* (student answers: plural), *Voici leurs livres* (student answers: singular/plural).

Interference of English speech habits appears in the student's pronunciation of French and use of French syntax rather than in the realm of morphology. There is, however, one important instance of English interference which must be mentioned in the present context, namely the danger of the student's equating French *sa* with her and French *son* with his. The fact that the French possessive agrees only with the noun it modifies must of course be made clear and the student must be put through extensive drills in which masculine possessors "possess" feminine nouns, and in which feminine possessors are associated with masculine nouns: *Jean cherche sa cravate, il met sa chemise: Jeanne met son chapeau, Elle fait son devoir.*

(C) THE ADJECTIVE AND THE ADVERB

French adjectives and nouns share many characteristics: both can have masculine and feminine forms (*bon chanteur/bonne chanteuse*); both can be used in some of the same syntactical positions (*il est intelligent/il est chanteur*). The only major difference which allows us to assign words to one class rather than to the other lies in the fact that from adjectives we can form adverbs, or that adjectives can at least be used adverbially (*il parle intelligemment: il parle haut*), while genuine nouns are incapable of adverb formation or adverbial use.

Just like nouns, adjectives usually do not indicate the singular/plural contrast in spoken French. The only exception to this principle occurs (1) with some adjectives that have special plural forms (*national/nationaux*), or (2) if the adjective stands before a noun beginning with a vowel (*petit enfant*/pətitãfã/: *petits enfants* /pətizãfã/).

The regular adjectives of French may be presented in two major groups: in the first group the masculine/feminine contrast is not expressed in speech: *noir; noire* /nwaʀ/, *public; publique* /pyblik/, *riche; riche* /ʀiʃ/, et cetera. With some of these adjectives there is of course an *orthographic* differentiation between masculine and feminine, as in two of the preceding examples, or in *pareil/pareille*.

The other large group of regular French adjectives differentiates the masculine from the feminine through the fact that the feminine forms end in a consonant or consonant group not heard in the masculine. In orthography this difference is normally presented by the masculine dropping the final *e* of the feminine form: *petite* /ptit/ vs. *petit* /pti/; *heureuse* /œRøz/ vs. *heureux* /œRø/ *distincte* /distɛ̃kt/ vs. *distinct* /distɛ̃/. Several important facts should be noted in connection with this rule: (1) Many of the adjectives which are irregular from the point of view of *orthography* are perfectly regular in oral French: *blanche* /blɑ̃ʃ/ vs. *blanc* /blɑ̃/; *fraîche* /fRɛʃ/ vs. *frais* /fRɛ/, *douce* /dus/ vs. *doux* /du/, *longue* /lɔ̃g/ vs. *long* /lɔ̃/. (2) With the dropping of the final consonant the preceding vowel will now appear in an open syllable: this means that /ɔ/ or /ɛ/ of the feminine appear as /o/ or /e/ in the masculine: *sotte* /sɔt/ vs. *sot* /so/, *première* /pRamjɛR/ vs. *premier* /pRamje/. (3) If the final consonant of the feminine form is a nasal consonant, the masculine form ends in a nasal vowel: *fine* /fin/ vs. *fin* /fɛ̃/, *pleine* /plɛn/ vs. *plein* /plɛ̃/, *maligne* /maliɲ/ vs. *malin* /malɛ̃/, *bonne* /bɔn/ vs. *bon* /bɔ̃/, *commune* /kɔmyn/ vs. *commun* /kɔmœ̃/.

In spoken French we may classify as irregular all those adjectives in which (1) masculine and feminine forms end in different consonants, as in *active* /aktiv/ vs. *actif* /aktif/, *sèche* /sɛʃ/ vs. *sec* /sɛk/, and (2) those in which the final /-l/ of the feminine does not appear in the masculine and in which the vowel preceding the /-l/ is changed: *belle* /bɛl/ vs. *beau* /bo/, *molle* /mɔl/ vs. *mou* /mu/, *folle* /fɔl/ vs. *fou* /fu/, *nouvelle* /nuvɛl/ vs. *nouveau* /nuvo/, (3) *vieille* /vjɛj/ vs. *vieux* /vjø/.

The behavior of adjectives in the position before nouns beginning with a vowel must be singled out for special treatment: many of the adjectives which normally differentiate masculine and feminine do not do so in oral French before singular nouns beginning with a vowel and use only the feminine form in that position: *petit ami* /ptit ami/ vs. *petite amie* /ptit ami/. The irregular adjectives, such as *beau, fou, vieux, nouveau*, follow this same pattern since they have special forms used before masculine words beginning with a vowel. These special forms in fact are, in oral French, identical with the feminine: *un bel arbre* vs. *une belle amie, un vieil ami* vs. *une vieille femme*. Many of the adjectives which have feminine forms ending in nasal consonants follow the same pattern. In speech, it is the feminine rather than the masculine form which appears before a vowel: *bon* /bɔ̃/ *livre* but *bon* /bɔn/ *enfant*, *ancien* /ɑ̃sjɛ̃/ *professeur* but *ancien* /ɑ̃sjɛn/ *ami*. This pattern of the masculine/feminine contrast not being distinguished before nouns beginning with a vowel should be pointed out to the student since it includes some of the most frequently used adjectives including the irregular ones such as *beau-bel-belle*, *vieux-vieil-vieille*.

There are, of course, several types of adjectives which do distinguish masculine/feminine forms before vowels. These are (1) the adjectives which distinguish the masculine from the feminine by using a voiced consonant as the ending in the feminine, as in *grand* /gʀɑ̃t/ *ami* vs. *grande* /gʀɑ̃d/ *amie*; (2) the adjectives in which the masculine form appears before vowels with a final /-z/ represented by *-x* in orthography and is pronounced in *liaison* as in *faux* /foz/ *ami* vs. *fausses* /fosz/ *idées*; (3) those adjectives ending in nasals which do distinguish feminine and masculine singular forms before vowels, as in *commun* /kɔmœ̃n/ *effort* vs. *commune* /kɔmyn/ *idée*. But with the possible exception of *grand* the adjectives which differentiate singular masculine and feminine prevocalic forms are quite rare, at least in the position before the noun.

The masculine/feminine contrast of adjectives can be drilled in exercises in which different nouns are substituted into the same pattern, as in *voici une étudiante intelligente*, substituting *un étudiant*, *une jeune fille*, *un professeur*, et cetera. The substitution nouns can be simply named by the teacher or they can be suggested by pictures or objects. Special care must be taken to point out the special plural forms or masculine singular forms which appear in the prevocalic position. Patterns like (a) *l'arbre est vieux* or *les arbres sont vieux* must be contrasted with (b) *ce sont de vieux arbres* or *c'est un vieil arbre*. The student might be asked to shift a series of sentences from pattern (a) to pattern (b) or vice versa: (Teacher) *est-ce que cet homme est vieux?* (Student) *Oui, c'est un vieil homme:* (Teacher) *Est-ce que l'enfant est bon?* (Student) *Oui, c'est un bon enfant:* (Teacher) *Est-ce que l'oiseau est beau?* (Student) *Oui, c'est un bel oiseau:* (Teacher) *Est-ce que ces hommes sont vieux?* (Student) *Oui, ce sont des vieux hommes:* (Teacher) *Est-ce que ces enfants sont bons?* (Student) *Oui, ce sont des bons enfants.*

The morphology of the regular adverb formation presents no particular problem: the ending *-ment* /mɑ̃/ is added to the feminine form, as in *franche* > *franchement* /fʀɑ̃ʃ/ > /fʀɑ̃ʃmɑ̃/; *heureuse* > *heureusement* /œʀø/ > /œʀøzmɑ̃/, et cetera. The irregular adverbs include (1) the adverbs of all the adjectives ending in /ɑ̃/, represented as *-ant*, *-ent* in orthography, which loses its nasality when the regular /mɑ̃/ suffix is added: *constant* > *constamment* /kɔ̃stɑ̃/ > /kɔ̃stamɑ̃/, *ardent* > *ardemment*

/aʀdã/ > /aʀdamã/; (2) the adverbs which are formed by the ending /emã/, as in *precise* > *précisément* /pʀesiz/ > /presizemã/, *énorme* > *énormément* /enɔʀm/ > /enɔʀmemã/, et cetera; (3) adverbs which are formed on a stem slightly different from that of the adjectives as in *bref, brève* > *brièvement, gentil, gentille* > *gentiment*; (4) adverbs which are formed on a completely different stem from the adjectives, such as *bon/bien, meilleur/mieux, mal/mauvais, pire/pis;* (5) adverbs which are completely identical with the corresponding adjectives, such as *haut, fort, bas*, as in *il chante haut, il parle bas.*

The formation of adverbs from adjectives is best drilled in a context, for instance in substitution exercises in which the teacher suggests adjectives which the student must transform into adverbs in order to use them in a sentence. Thus the teacher may suggest adjectives like *lent, rapide, courant, bon* which the student changes to adverbs and fits into a sentence like *je parle français; je parle français lentement, je parle français rapidement, je parle français couramment, je parle bien français.*

(D) THE VERB

The teaching of the verb forms is naturally one of the chief problems for the French teacher. Not only is the entire concept of conjugational endings difficult for the speaker of English, but the irregular patterns within French make its verbal system fairly complicated. In support of a purely oral course, or at least an initially oral presentation, it can be said that the written French conjugational system is quite a bit more complex than the oral. In the latter, for instance, the singular forms within the present or imperfect are the same, with the exception of the present tense of the verbs *aller, être, avoir*, and a few forms produced only in liaison. In written French the past participle appears in the singular and plural and in masculine and feminine forms: *connu (s)– connue (s)*, whereas in oral French there is usually no distinction between these forms unless the feminine form ends in a consonant in speech: feminine, *écrite* /ekʀit/, masculine, *écrit* /ekʀi/.

In any French course it is advisable to start the teaching of the verb with a basic form from which the others can be derived, step by step, always making a single change. The most logical forms to be used as the base are probably the third or the first person plural. The infinitive is not particularly suitable as the base on which to build different forms for linguistic as well as purely pedagogical reasons. It does not serve as basis for as many forms as do the plurals of the present indicative and it is functionally less useful. In the initial stages of the course it is easy enough to describe what the Frenchmen or Americans (or French children) are doing (third person plural) or discuss what we do in class or elsewhere (first person plural), but how can one use the infinitives often enough to make them the secure functional base for further operations? From the purely theoretical point of view the present participle (*finissant, comprenant*) could also serve as a base form, but in practice it is useless because of its comparatively infrequent use. In addition, the present participle opens up a rich source of errors (giving the student the opportunity to furnish literal translations of such expressions as I am going, or after leaving). Thus for purely practical and pedagogical reasons it should be introduced in the basic course as late rather than as early as possible.

No matter how we proceed in the study of the verbs, there will always be irregular patterns or forms which have to be learned as exceptions. Depending on the sequence with which we study the forms (third person plural as base, or first person plural as base) different forms will have to be classified as irregular. The best approach is the one that (1) yields a minimum of irregularities and (2) which bases the teaching of verbs on those forms which are most useful and frequent in speech and which can, therefore, be most easily and naturally retained by the student.

The following is a suggested "outline map" according to which the verb could be taught. Again the analysis is based on the spoken language with the assumption that it will be taught first and that the habit formation will take place in speech rather than in writing. The analysis is in turn based on a linguistic principle that seems pedagogically useful in this particular case—namely, that a pattern can be presented in terms of **successive transformations** starting from a base form. There are, of course, other possible approaches. For instance, in our analysis we may differentiate quite clearly all the morphemic elements involved in a verb form: a form like *chanterons* /ʃɑ̃tRɔ̃/ seems to break up into a root /ʃɑ̃t/, which carries the semantic meaning of the verb, and the ending /Rɔ̃/ which expresses first person plural future. But if we compare *chanterons* /ʃɑ̃tRɔ̃/ with *chantons* /ʃɑ̃tɔ̃/, *chantions* /ʃɑ̃tjɔ̃/, we find that we can isolate /ɔ̃/ as expressing first person plural while /r/ is the element which indicates future: /ʃɑ̃tɔ̃/ (*chantons*) vs. /ʃɑ̃tRɔ̃/ (*chanterons*). Thus *chanterons* actually breaks down into a **root**, a **tense sign**, and a **personal ending**. There is perhaps some pedagogical merit to this type of analysis (point out to the student that /r/ is a future marker); but from the viewpoint of teaching the production of the tenses, it is hardly advisable to break down the verb into more than two elements, one element which carries the semantic meaning (the root or base) and another which carries the grammatical meaning (tense and/or person). Of course in many cases tense will also be signaled by a change in the base, by the formation of a **special future stem** (as in *saurai*) or past stem (*su, sus*). But, as stated before, rather than presenting a precise linguistic dissection, we are offering an outline of successive changes:

Step 1.   The base form from which the others are taught is the **third person plural present**: parlent /paRl/, finissent /finis/, vendent /vãd/.

Step 2.   Formation of the **third person singular present**: according to the relation of the third person singular to the third person plural, French verbs may be divided into two general classes:

I.   Those verbs in which the **third person singular** sounds like the third person plural **(the first conjugation verbs)**: *il parle* /il paRl/, *ils parlent* /il paRl/.

II.   Those verbs which use a shortened base form for the third person singular present. This shortened base is formed by dropping the final consonant of the third person plural: *ils finissent* /il finis/, *il finit* /il fini/; *ils vendent* /ilvãd/, *il vend* /il vã/.

The above pattern is true for all the regular -*ir* and -*re* verbs and the majority of the irregular verbs:

ils partent	/paRt/ >	*il part*	/paR/
ils doivent	/dwav/	*il doit*	/dwa/
ils servent	/sɛRv/	*il sert*	/sɛR/

In some cases the disappearance of the final consonant of the third person plural is accompanied by predictable changes in the vowel. If the final consonant is a nasal /n/ or /ɲ/, the third person plural form will end in a nasal vowel. To be more specific, /ɛɲ/ becomes /ɛ̃/ as in *craignent* > *craint*, *peignent* > *peint*; /ɛn/ becomes /ɛ̃/ as in *viennent* > *vient*, *tiennent* > *tient*; /aɲ/ becomes /ɛ̃/ as in *poignent* > *point*. If the third person plural form contains /œ/, then it will become /ø/, the closed vowel, as in *veulent/veut, peuvent/peut*.

The verbs which are completely irregular in the third person singular-plural relationship are *être* (*sont/est*), *faire* (*font/fait*), *aller* (*vont/va*), *savoir* (*savent/sait*), *valoir* (*valent/vaut*), and also *prendre* (*prennent/prend*) in which the singular appears with /ã/ rather than with the /ɛ̃/ which we could expect on the basis of the above mentioned pattern of *viennent/vient.*

Step 3.   **The first and second person singular present** is identical with the third person singular:

> il parle   :   je parle, tu parles   /paʀl/
> il finit   :   je finis, tu finis   /fini/
> il vend   :   je vends, tu vends   /vã/

The only exceptions to this pattern are the verbs *être* (*je suis, tu es*), *aller* (*je vais, tu vas*), *avoir* (*j'ai, tu as*).

Step 4.   **The first person plural present** is the third person plural, followed by /ɔ̃/:

> ils finissent   /finis/   >   nous finissons   /finisɔ̃/
> ils parlent   /paʀl/   >   nous parlons   /paʀlɔ̃/
> ils vendent   /vãd/   >   nous vendons   /vãdɔ̃/
> ils écrivent   /ekʀiv/   >   nous écrivons   /ekʀivɔ̃/

It is, of course, in this particular step that most of the irregularities occur. Some of these follow certain predictable or nearly predictable patterns. Thus verbs of class I which have /ɛ/ in the base usually change to /ə/ or zero in the first person plural: *ils achètent* /aʃɛt/ > *nous achetons* /aʃtɔ̃/, *ils lèvent* /lɛv/ > *nous levons* /lvɔ̃/. But *ils préfèrent* /prefɛʀ/ > *nous préférons* /preferɔ̃/ shows that /ɛ/ > /e/ is also a possible alternation.

Other irregular verbs may be grouped according to the vowel alternation involved in the change: /œ/ > /u/ as in *veulent* > *voulons, peuvent* > *pouvons*; /ɛ/ > /ə/ as in *prennent* > *prenons*; /jɛ/ > /ə/ as in *viennent* > *venons, tiennent* > *tenons*; /wa/ > /ə/ as in *reçoivent* > *recevons*; /wa/ > /y/ as in *boivent* > *buvons*. Note also that /j/ appears in the first person plural when the third person plural ends in a vowel, as in *voient* /vwa/ > *voyons* /vwajɔ̃/. We may classify as completely irregular those verbs in which more than an alternation of the vowel of the base is involved in the change from third person plural to first person plural: *sont/sommes, font/faisons, ont/avons, vont/allons.*

Step 5.   **The second person plural present** is derived from the first person by substituting the ending *-ez* /e/ for the ending *-ons* /ɔ̃/.

> finissons   >   finissez
> avons   >   avez

There are only three exceptions to this rule: the verbs which form the second person plural in /t/: *êtes, dites, faites.*

Step 6.   **The singular and the third person plural of the imperfect** are formed by substituting the end /ɛ/ (often /e/ in colloquial French) for the /ɔ̃/ or /e/ of the first or second person present.

Nous prenons	/pRənɔ̃/	> *je prenais*	/pRənɛ/
		> *tu prenais*	/pRənɛ/
		il prenait	/pRənɛ/
		ils prenaient	/pRənɛ/

The only verb which does not follow this pattern is *être* (*nous sommes* > *j'étais*).

Step 7.   **The first and second person plural imperfect** are formed by substituting the ending /jɔ̃/ and /je/ for the /ɛ/ of the singular (or by interpolating the sound /j/ before the endings /ɔ̃/ and /e/ of the corresponding forms of the present).

Je prenais	/pRənɛ/	> *nous prenions*	/pRənjɔ̃/
		vous preniez	/pRənje/

This pattern has no exceptions. If the endings /jɔ̃/ and /je/ are added to a base ending in two consonants such as in *rentr-ais* /Rɑ̃tRɛ/, they become dissyllabic /ijɔ̃/ and /ije/ in order to avoid the coming together of three consonants: hence, *rentrions* /Rɑ̃tRijɔ̃/, *perdiez* /pɛRdije/. If the base preceding the ending has a variant in which the two consonants are separated by /ə/, it is the latter which is commonly used before /jɔ̃/ and /je/; thus *achetais* /aʃtɛ/ but *achetions* /aʃətjɔ̃/, *levais* /lvɛ/ but *levions* /ləvjɔ̃/.

Step 8.   **The future** is formed by adding the endings /Re/ (first person singular, second person plural), /Ra/ (second person singular and third person singular), /Rɔ̃/ /first and third person plural) to the singular form of the present:

Je trouve	/tRuv/	> *je trouverai*	/tRuvRe/

Je finis	/fini/	*je finirai*	/finiRe/
J'écris	/ekRi/	*j'écrirai*	/ekRiRe/
Je ris	/Ri/	*je rirai*	/RiRe/
Je cours	/kuR/	*je courrai*	/kuRRe/

But there we note that /əRe/ rather than /Re/ is used if the stem ends in

two consonants, as in *je parle* /paRl/ > *je parlerai* /paRləRe/. The same is
true if the stem ends in a vowel: *je crée* /kRe/ > *je créerai* /kReəRe/.

The usual approach to the teaching of the future is to take the
infinitive as the base form. Yet from the viewpoint of oral French
there are several objections against this approach, even if the infinitive
form has been taught already by the time the future tense is presented.
The association of infinitive and future tense is apt to produce wrong
forms, especially with verbs like *acheter, appeler, jeter*. The future of
these verbs (*achèterai, appellerai, jetterai*) is formed by adding the *-rai*
/Re/ ending to the singular of the present. Both future and present singular contain the same base form with open *e* /ɛ/, the latter being orthographically indicated either by the *accent grave* or the doubling of the
following consonant. Even with verbs like *finir*, or *tomber*, the student
who is forming the future by adding to the infinitive is likely to produce
forms like /tɔ̃ bəRe/ instead of /tɔ̃bRe/, /finir-e/ instead of /finiRe/. On
the other hand, there are also disadvantages involved in not approaching
the future through the infinitive, since there are quite a few verbs in
which the rule *future = present* + /Re/ will not work, while *infinitive* + /e/
does, such as *vendre, connaître, prendre*. There are also verbs like *préférer,
espérer* in which, in standard French at least, the future shows the *é* /e/ of
the infinitive rather than the *è* /ɛ/ of the present: *je préférerai* vs. *je préfère*.

Several solutions are possible for the teaching of such irregularities.
The teaching of these future forms may have to be postponed until
the infinitives are presented; or many of these verbs may be presented
as special groups in which the future is formed by the form /dRe/ rather
than /Re/ if the singular stem of present ends in a nasal vowel:
viens /vjɛ̃/ *viendrai* /vjɛ̃dRe/, *prends* /pRɑ̃/ *prendrai* /pRɑ̃dRe/, *attends*
/atɑ̃/ *attendrai* /atɑ̃dRe/, *vends* /vɑ̃/ *vendrai* /vɑ̃dRe/, *crains* /kRɛ̃/ *craindrai*
/kRɛ̃dRe/. This grouping does not, of course, take care of verbs such
as *sentir, mentir, dormir, rompre*. These form yet another group, if we
teach the future based on the present singular form: *je sens* /sɑ̃/ > *je
sentirai* /sɑ̃tiRe/.

Those verbs which have irregular special future stems, such as *je
saurai, je voudrai, je pourrai, je verrai, je serai, j'aurai, je mourrai,
j'enverrai, je recevrai, je ferai, j'irai, il pleuvra, je voudrai*, will always
remain irregular no matter what system we may use to explain the
formation of the future tense. It is, however, to be noted that some of
the so-called irregular verbs such as *courir, s'asseoir* can become regular
if the present is used as base: *je cours* /kuR/ > *je courrai* /kuRRe/, *je
m'assieds* /asje/ > *je m'assiérai* /asjeRe/.

Step 9.   **The conditional** is formed from the future by replacing the final vowels of the future with the endings used in the imperfect:

Je lirai	/liʀe/	*je lirais*	/liʀɛ/
		tu lirais	/liʀɛ/
		il lirait	/liʀɛ/
		ils liraient	/liʀɛ/
		nous lirions	/liʀjɔ̃/
		vous liriez	/liʀje/

We must note (a) that the endings /jɔ̃/ and /je/ become disyllabic (/ijɔ̃/ and /ije/) after two consonants, as in *prendrions* /pʀɑ̃dʀijɔ̃/, *vendriez* /vɑ̃dʀije/; (b) that in verbs of Class I (*-er* ending verbs) /ə/ appears before these two endings, as in *trouverions* /tʀuvəʀjɔ̃/, *chercheriez* /ʃɛʀʃəʀje/, et cetera; (c) that /ə/ appears in the stem before these endings to avoid the following together of three consonants: *nous serions* /səʀjɔ̃/, *vous seriez* /səʀje/, but *je serai* /sʀe/.

Step 10.   **The present subjunctive singular and third person plural** are identical with the third person plural of the present indicative.

Ils prennent	/pʀɛn/	*je prenne*	/pʀɛn/
		tu prennes	/pʀɛn/
		il prenne	/pʀɛn/
		ils prennent	/pʀɛn/
Ils boivent	/bwav/	*je boive*	/bwav/
		tu boives	/bwav/
		il boive	/bwav/
		ils boivent	/bwav/

There are only a few exceptions to this rule, *faire* (*fasse*), *savoir* (*sache*), *pouvoir* (*puisse*), *aller* (*aille*), *avoir* (*aie*), *vouloir* (*veuille*), *valoir* (*vaille*), *être* (*sois*).

Step 11.   **The first and second person plural subjunctive** are identical with the corresponding imperfect forms. The only exceptions are *pouvoir* (*puissions*), *faire* (*fassions*), *savoir* (*sachions*), *être* (*soyons*), and *avoir* (*ayons*). It is to be noted that the subjunctive forms of *aller*, *vouloir*, *valoir*, which are irregular in the singular and third person plural, conform to the regular patterns in the first and second person plural: *il faut que vous y* **alliez**, *il est important que nous* **voulions** *le faire*, and so on.

Step 12. **The imperatives** are identical with the second person singular and plural, and first person plural of the present indicative: *parle!* (note the orthographic absence of *-s*), *parlez!*, *parlons!* Although in this scheme we mention the imperative as a late step, they can be taught early in any course. The only exceptions to be noted are *avoir, être, savoir, vouloir,* which form their imperative on their irregular subjunctive stems.

Step 13. **The infinitive** of all Class I verbs is the base form followed by /e/, represented in orthography by *-er*, as in *parlent* /paʀl/ > *parler* /paʀle/. The other regular verbs may be split into two main groups: those in which the infinitive is the third person plural + r (*vendent* /vãd/ > *vendre* /vãdʀ/) and those in which the infinitive is the shortened singular base + r (*finit* /fini/ > *finir* /finiʀ/).

Another possibility is to present a formula, infinitive = singular present + /dʀ/, for all verbs ending in a nasal vowel, as in *attend* /atã/ > *attendre* /atãdʀ/, *prend* /pʀã/ > *prendre* /pʀãdʀ/, *craint* /kʀɛ̃/ > *craindre* /kʀɛ̃dʀ/. Again, certain verbs such as *sentir, mentir, rompre,* will not follow this rule and will have to be treated with verbs like *connaître, tenir, venir, devoir,* as irregular infinitives.

Step 14. **The past participle** can be taught as identical in sound with the infinitive for all Class I verbs (*parler* > *parlé*), or as base form + /e/ (*parlent* > *parlé*). The past participle of the other verbs can be presented as base + /y/ (*vendent* /vãd/ *vendu* /vãdy/) or as identical with the shortened singular base for the type *finit* /fini/ > *fini* /fini/. This presentation does not solve the problem of all the verbs which have their own irregular past participle stems. They must be learned as irregular forms, perhaps best in certain groupings. The irregular past participles ending in /y/ form one such group (*vu, dû, su, lu,* et cetera), the past participle in /i/ form another (*mis, pris, assis,* et cetera).

Step 15. **The present participle** can be formed from the first person plural present by replacing the /ɔ̃/ ending by /ã/, as in *lisons* /lizɔ̃/ > *lisant* /lizã/. Exceptions are *étant, ayant,* and *sachant.*

Step 16. **The "literary" tenses of French (past definite and imperfect subjunctive** and their compound tenses) should be approached from the viewpoint of the written, rather than the spoken system. Most likely, they will not be taught until other tenses have been practiced in speech as well as in orthography. Thus the conventional approach of teaching the recognition of written endings seems fully justified here and there seems no need to present a detailed analysis of these tenses. The teaching of the irregular past definite and imperfect subjunctive can be approached best from the irregular past participles. Most verbs which have the past participle ending in /y/ keep the /y/ in the past definite form, as in *dû*, *je dus*; *eu*, *j'eus*. Most verbs having /i/ in the past participle will also retain that sound in the past definite, as in *mis*, *je mis*; *pris*, *je pris*. Explained in this way, there will be only a few exceptions, such as *vu* vs. *je vis*, *tenu* vs. *je tins*. There are some completely unpredictable forms such as *je mourus*, *je fus*, *je naquis*, *je fis*, which must be presented as a special group.

While we presented the verb patterns by a series of successive trans- formations, shifting from one tense or person to another should not be the *only* exercise with which to drill verb forms. The typical problem for the student who is producing a French sentence is that after choosing the subject such as *je*, *nous*, *mon père*, he is faced with the problem of finding the matching verb form. If he has been drilled only with trans- formation drills, of the type *nous parlons > vous parlez*, *nous com- prenons > vous comprenez*, he may be in almost the same situation as the student who has been brought up in old-fashioned conjugations and who has to recite *je vais*, *tu vas*, *il va*, *nous allons*, *vous allez*, in order to remember the third person plural *vont*. The student should not have to go through a series of transformation and shifting exercises in order to be able to produce a correct form. What we must teach the student is not merely the derivation but above all the instantaneous use of verb forms. Derivations are crutches of linguistic description or pedagogical presentation. After the student has been introduced to the correct forms he must still be put through exercises which force him to use these forms automatically. Thus we may ask the student to change the subject of a simple sentence: *Je reçois la lettre;* substitute in this sentence *nous*, *vous*, *mes amis*, and so forth. We may adapt transforma- tion exercises into meaningful conversational patterns. For instance, the shift from the second person (plural) to the first person is a "natural" pattern of conversational exchange: *Est-ce que vous me comprenez? Oui, je vous comprends.* We may also suggest different subjects and tenses for action pictures of the type described in our section on visual aids: we point to the picture showing a man waiting for the bus and say *Hier nous . . ., demain nous . . .,* and expect the student to complete the sentence with *hier nous avons attendu l'autobus, demain nous attendrons l'autobus.*

One aspect of French morphology not covered in detail in our presentation concerns the **forms of the pronouns**. We shall merely mention a few aspects of pronoun morphology which seem pedagogically important. The unstressed personal pronouns (just as the negative *ne*) are, of course, "bound forms." Just as the determinatives are satellites of the noun, they are satellites of the verb, without which they cannot exist. For the student, the most difficult problem connected with the use of personal pronouns is their sequence and position—a syntactical rather than a morphological problem. The syntactical and morphological aspects are, in a sense, inseparable: the position of the pronoun often determines the morphological variant, the allomorph, that must be used. Again it is important to realize that these variants should be drilled as different forms rather than as different pronunciations of the same form. Obviously the prevocalic variants must be contrasted in special drills: *Est-ce qu'il trouve le livre? Oui, il le* /lə/ *trouve:* but *Est-ce qu'il admire le livre? Oui, il l'* /l/ *admire: Est-ce qu'il trouve les livres? Oui, il les* /le/ *trouve: Est-ce qu'il admire les livres? Oui, il les* /lez/ *admire.* Or the student may be drilled in the use of the variants by the substitution of different verbs: *Il nous* /nu/ *regarde,* substitute *admire*: *Il nous* /nuz/ *admire.* Special drills on singular/plural recognition should center on the third person of the verb. With the *-re* and *-ir* verbs the difference between singular and plural present is, as stated before, orally conveyed by the verb ending (*vendent* /vãd/, *vend* /vã/, *finissent* /finis/ *finit* /fini/). But with *-er* verbs in the present, or with all verbs in the imperfect, the subject pronoun takes over this function whenever it stands before a vowel: /ilpaʀl/ or /ilpaʀlɛ/ may be singular or plural, but /ilzaʀiv/ or /ilzaʀivɛ/ are clearly marked as plurals by the /ilz/ variant of the pronoun. Drills in which the student is asked to identify forms like *il vend, ils vendent, il arrive, ils arrivent,* as singular or plural will teach him rather rapidly to observe and to produce the essential grammatical signals.

To say that the personal pronouns or *ne* are bound forms means that in a sense they are just prefixes or affixes of the verb. Pedagogically they should be treated as such. This means that sequences like /ʒən/ in *je ne sais pas* /ʒənsɛpɑ/ or /məl/ in *il me le donne* /ilməldɔn/ must be learned as complete units which can be put before various verbs. Intellectual "assembly" by the student is a slow process doomed to failure: /ʒən/, /məl/ or /ləlɥi/, must be drilled as units in patterns in which they remain constant while the rest of the sentence changes:

Est-ce qu'il vous donne le livre? Oui, il me le /məl/ *donne; Est-ce qu'il vous rend le livre? Oui, il me le* /məl/ *rend; Est-ce qu'il vous vend le livre? Oui, il me le* /məl/ *vend.*

(E) WORD DERIVATION

In our discussion of morphemes we have so far distinguished between **roots**, those elements which carry the vocabulary meanings, and grammatical **morphenes**, which carry the structural or grammatical meaning. Yet there is still a third type of building stone which may be used in various circumstances with the same identifiable meaning, namely the various prefixes and suffixes which are used in word formation or derivation: the *-eur* /œʀ/ which can be combined with a root such as *chant* /ʃɑ̃t/ to form *chanteur* /ʃɑ̃tœʀ/, and which is used again with the same meaning of "noun of agency" in *fumeur, défenseur, amateur*; or the prefix *im-, in-* /ɛ̃/ denoting negation, which appears in *impossible, injuste, intolérable.*

Word derivation has little if any pedagogical application in the initial stages of the audio-lingual course. Whether any given prefix or suffix can be added to a specific root is not predictable; in other words, the existence of *table* and *-eur* does not allow us to assume that there is a word **"tableur."** But in the vocabulary building phase of the course and in the teaching of reading it is quite essential that the student become familiar with the meaning of derivational suffixes and prefixes. This knowledge will enable him to guess correctly within a context the meaning of innumerable words which would otherwise send him to the dictionary.

The teaching of derivation suffixes or prefixes can be approached in two complementary ways: either through the teaching of "word families" (words formed on the same root) or the teaching of series of words formed with the same derivational morpheme. Thus the meaning of *-oir* can be made clear by teaching to the student a word series like *dortoir, abattoir, lavoir*, and then inviting him to guess the meaning of *parloir* and *fumoir*. Or a series like *jaunir, rougir, brunir*, can be presented in sentences in context, preparing the way for other sentences in which the student guesses the meaning of *noircir*, and *rembrunir*. In the word family approach, the student is presented with sentences which use the family in a meaningful context. *On achète des patins pour patiner. Celui qui patine est patineur. J'aime le patinage.* The bibliography contains references to texts in which this method is employed in vocabulary teaching. Basically, it represents the extension of the pattern practice approach to vocabulary learning. Since many of the French derivational suffixes and prefixes have recognizable English counterparts, we shall again touch upon the problem of derivation in the discussion of cognates in vocabulary recognition.

CHAPTER VIII

Teaching Syntactical Patterns

(A) THE BASIC PATTERN OF FRENCH: NOUN AND VERB CLUSTERS

Derivational, lexical and grammatical morphemes combine into larger units—words. The purpose of syntactical analysis is to determine just how words can be used and combined to make up larger units of speech such as phrases, clauses, sentences. There are several methods of approaching the syntactical analysis of a language. The details of procedure and the relative merits of these methods deserve mention insofar as they have an obvious relation to teaching procedures. Thus one method of syntactical analysis consists of dividing an utterance into those elements which seem to be the basic constructions (usually two) of which the utterance is made up. These constructions which are referred to as the **immediate constituents** of the utterance are then in turn divided into **their own immediate constituents.** Thus a sentence like "My sister's husband speaks French quite fluently" divides into two immediate constituents: (1) "my sister's husband," (2) "speaks French quite fluently." The first immediate constituent, "my sister's husband," has in turn the immediate constituents "my sister's" and "husband." Another approach to syntactical analysis emphasizes the fact that syntactical units are related if they fill the same "slot" in an utterance. Thus every syntactical unit is defined not only by its own makeup, but also by the position which it can fill in a larger utterance. These types of syntactical analysis have an obvious relationship to the expansion and substitution exercises. In the former, the student is given a small sentence like *Mon ami est arrivé* and is then asked to expand this structure by successively adding elements like *ce soir, avec son oncle, à huit heures, pour nous parler.* It has been pointed out before that the substitution exercise is basically a principle of analysis converted into a teaching method.

Another type of syntactical analysis is based on the concept that the entire syntax of a language can be described in formulas showing how certain utterances can be created from others by successive series of transformations. Still another approach starts from the premise that one of the necessary constituent elements of any syntactical unit is an intonation pattern, and that the surest way of identifying the component elements of any utterance is through the study and isolation of such intonation patterns. Both approaches mentioned have pedagogical implications: the transformation approach opens up the possibility of teaching the entire syntax of language through transformation exercises; the emphasis on the intonation pattern reminds us that such intonation patterns must be taught as integral parts of the utterance, and that in French the stress and breath groups which we have mentioned in Chapter V are not only phonetic but also syntactical units of French.

There are at present no exhaustive analyses of French using any one of the methods just described. Yet whatever method we may want to employ, the most essential facts concerning French syntax are fairly obvious. Let us approach them by taking another look at the concept of "word" which we have used in our definition of syntax. We all would readily call *les, ne, pas, aujourd'hui, lui, ami, volonté, mon,* "words" and consider them as the units or building stones out of which syntactical constructions are made up. But our reasons for calling all these units words is, basically, that they are listed as such in the dictionary, and that they are different from each other in spelling. If we consider the fact of oral language alone, the concept of word becomes quite difficult to define. Linguists have tried different approaches. One way to define words is to ask a native speaker to pronounce connected utterances in such a way that he makes a pause within these utterances whenever such pauses would seem plausible to him. All the segments marked off by pauses could then be called words. Another way of getting at the definition of word is to call it a "minimum free form." This means a form that could stand as an utterance by itself in actual speech. The important implication of these definitions in analysis of French syntax lies not so much in the theoretical aspects concerning the definition of word, but in the fairly obvious fact that according to the above definition *ne, mon, le, pas*, could certainly not qualify as words: no one could make a pause after *ne, le* in *je ne le sais pas*, or after *mon* in *mon ami*, nor is it possible to make an utterance like *mon* or *le*, except perhaps in answer to a question about French grammar. Now, whether we call *mon, le, ne, pas*, words or suffixes or bound forms ("bound" because they cannot occur by themselves) does not matter too much. The fact is that their usage indicates that there are in French certain "words" like *mon, ce, le* (the determinatives) which are indeed "bound" to the noun, and others like *y, en, me, te, ne*, which are bound to the verb. We called the former the satellites of the noun, the latter the satellites of the verb. Most French utterances are thus made up of **noun and verb constructions or clusters**. Each noun or verb cluster has a center which is the noun or verb itself. Around this center are the noun or verb satellites and/or other free forms such as adjectives and adverbs modifying the nucleus.

Notre ancien ami ne comprend pas les nouvelles ideés de votre professeur.
N (noun cluster)   v (verb cluster)   N (noun cluster)   N (noun cluster).

The typical basic structure of the French utterance is, of course, very much like English. The noun construction may be used without a preposition, in which case it functions either as subject, direct object, predicate nominative or appositive according to its position in the sentence, or it may be used after a preposition. In the latter case it becomes subordinate to either a noun or verb construction (*je parle* (v) *de mon ancien ami* (N); *le chapeau* (N) *de mon ancien ami* (N). The verb construction may also be used with or without preceding preposition and may become dependent on other verb or noun constructions (*il a décidé* (v) *de ne pas parler* (v); *il a pris* (v) *la décision* (N) *de ne pas parler* (v). Finally, there are some verb constructions which we may call **compound clusters**; like *il ne le lui avait pas* (v) *dit* (v).

With comparatively few exceptions, the main difficulties in French facing the speaker of English do not lie in the arrangement of the Noun and Verb clusters themselves, but rather within the formation of these clusters. The comparison of a few English and French sentences will bear this out:

Noun	*Verb*	*Noun*
Intelligent students	don't drink	wine.
Les étudiants intelligents	*ne boivent pas*	*de vin.*

The **noun-verb-noun pattern** is the same in both languages. The difficulties in French concern the use of the article for generalization and the position of the adjective in the first noun cluster, the formation of the negative in the verb cluster, the use of the partitive article in the second noun cluster. Let us compare another pair of sentences:

Verb	Verb	Noun
Without looking at him	he gave him	some money.
Sans le regarder	*il lui a donné*	*de l'argent.*

Again, there is overall similarity in the arrangement of the pattern: preposition-verb cluster, verb cluster, noun cluster. The difficulties are within each group; the use of the infinitive after the preposition in French, the position of the pronoun object, the use of the partitive.

The above examples do not mean to imply that the French and English parallelism in the position of nouns and verbs will hold true in all cases. But it underlines the fact that the initial task for the teacher and perhaps the most difficult, must be to teach the makeup of the noun and verb clusters themselves. In case of the noun clusters, this means above all (1) the use of the partitive article, (2) the use of the definite article for generalizations, (3) the position of the adjectives, (4) the formation and use of the determinatives. In case of the verb clusters, it means (1) the position of the pronouns, (2) the formation of the interrogative and (3) the formation of negative forms.

The student will never be able to produce French utterances with any degree of fluency or accuracy unless he can produce the compositive elements, the verbal and noun clusters, quickly and automatically. Noun clusters and verb clusters may be mentally arranged and assembled into sentences, but this process of arrangement and assembly cannot be applied to the clusters themselves. Phonetically and syntactically they are units by themselves. They are, so to speak, the "real" words which make up the French utterance. They are the units which must come to the speaker's mind already assembled and complete.

The student should of course have the analytic understanding of why a partitive is used in *je bois du café*, or why a certain sequence of pronouns occurs in *je ne le lui donne pas*, and another sequence in *je ne te le donne pas*. But this analytic understanding of the structure of the nucleus itself will at best make it possible for the student to construct the clusters laboriously for the purpose of passing a written examination. For the purpose of using them in speech there is no time for going through the construction process. There the clusters must become units which are readily and automatically available. The best way to insure this is to use them over and over again in sentences in which the complex cluster remains constant while other elements are being changed. For instance, we can ask the student to substitute different subjects in a sentence like *je mange du pain*, or *je cherche des étudiants intelligents*. While ostensibly drilling the different forms of the verb, the student is using the noun nucleus *du pain* or *des étudiants intelligents* over and over again and committing this construction to memory. We could achieve the same purpose by asking the student to substitute other verbs such as *achète, cherche, vends* in the first sentence, or we might even replace the noun itself by such words as *fromage, lait, beurre* in the first sentence; that is, change one item within the noun cluster but keep its total structure intact.

In the teaching of the verb cluster the above principle can be applied in the following way; for instance, we want to teach the verbal nucleus *je ne le lui ai pas* which is normally followed by another verb form like *donné* or *expliqué*. We set up an exercise in which the student is asked to answer questions, replacing nouns by pronouns:

> *Avez-vous lu la lettre à votre ami?*
> *Non, je ne la lui ai pas lue.*
> *Avez-vous écrit la lettre à votre ami?*
> *Non, je ne la lui ai pas écrite.*
> *Avez-vous expliqué la lettre à votre ami?*
> *Non, je ne la lui ai pas expliquée.*
> *Avez-vous envoyé la lettre à votre ami?*
> *Non, je ne la lui ai pas envoyée.*

In answering the question the student repeats *je ne la lui ai pas* over and over again. We are in fact going through a substitution exercise in which different past participles are being substituted in the same construction while the verbal cluster itself remains constant.

The above type of exercise should not be confused with the kind of drill that teaches the assembly of the cluster itself. If we ask the student to substitute different nouns like *crème, bière, café, alcool* in a pattern such as *je bois du vin*, we are directing his attention to the noun nucleus and teaching him to put it together. If we ask him to replace nouns by pronouns in sentences like *vous me donnez le livre* and *vous donnez le livre à Charles*, we are directing his attention to the verbal cluster and to the difference in word order between *vous me le donnez* and *vous le lui donnez*. These exercises are, of course, also useful and necessary. But unless they are eventually followed and supplemented by drills for the complete cluster, they may leave the student at the undesirable point where he must assemble each cluster out of its component elements.

Another important reason for teaching the complete clusters, rather than their assembly alone, is the fact that within the cluster the constituent elements appear in specific forms which do not exist outside of the clusters. We have already mentioned fixed units such as /ʒən/ as in *je ne le sais pas* and *je ne le comprends pas*. Another example comes from the formation of the interrogative forms of the verb. This form may, of course, be produced by putting the subject pronoun after the verb, as in *apprenez-vous?*, *cherchons-nous?*. In the third person, /t/ which is normally absent in the declarative form appears invariably in the interrogative:

Il apprend	/ilapʀɑ̃/	but	*Apprend-il*	/apʀɑ̃til/
Elle dit	/ɛldi/	but	*Dit-elle*	/ditɛl/
Ils savent	/ilsav/	but	*Savent-ils*	/savtil/
Il trouve	/iltʀuv/	but	*Trouve-t-il*	/tʀuvtil/
Il va	/ilva/	but	*Va-t-il*	/vatil/

This means that in oral French the interrogative of the third person contains a signal /til/ or /tɛl/ after the verb form. If the verb form ends in two consonants /ətil/ appears to avoid the coming together of three consonants, as in *parle-t-il?* /parlətil/. Whether the third person singular ends in orthography in a *t* as in *fait* or in a vowel as in *va* does not make any difference at all for the oral pattern. Now this kind of essential signal for the interrogative can be easily missed and will certainly not become a pattern of automatic recognition or production if the student learns about the interrogative form only through the analytic-synthetic process of "putting pronouns after the verb." Only exercises in which the complete third person interrogative verb cluster is used over and over will make the above pattern evident and a matter of automatic use.

(B) THE MECHANISM OF INTERFERENCE: DIFFERENCE OF MEDIA

It is not this book's purpose to give a complete analysis of French and English syntax showing all the structural differences which are

likely to cause trouble for the English speaker. We will content our-
selves with explaining the principles involved in such a comparison
and we shall cite the most important trouble spots as illustration.

One way of approaching the comparison between the structures of
two languages is to study the different ways in which structural relations
and meanings are expressed. So far in our discussion of syntax, we have
stressed only one of these, word order, which is perhaps most important
in English as well as in French. Another important medium for the
expression of structural meaning is the one that often does not appear
at all on the printed pages, intonation. We have already demonstrated
it in Chapter V, in comparing the difference between "White House"
and "white house." If we say "new White House" the structural relation
between new and White is not the same as in new white house. In the
latter new and white are both parallel modifiers of house, while in the
former we feel that new modifies the concept White House. To give
another example: *Charles apprend le français* with an up-down intonation
is a statement, but if we change this pattern of intonation the same
sentence becomes a question. To repeat, the intonation pattern is an
important signal, one of the necessary immediate constituents of any
utterance in both English and French.

Other important ways of signaling structural meaning and syntactical
relationship are **inflection** (government) and **agreement** (concord).
By inflection, we mean that any particular form indicates by itself its
relation to the others. The most typical example is the use of distinct
case endings. In the Latin sentence *puerum videt pater* we know that
pater is the subject of the sentence because of the ending alone, and
likewise we recognize *puerum* as the object of the sentence. By agreement,
we mean that an accord between forms (usually of endings) indicates
that these forms belong together. Again in the Latin sentence *bonum
videt pater puerum*, we know only because of the ending in *bonum* that
it modifies *puerum* rather than *pater*.

Both English and French utilize inflection and agreement. In English
we use different cases for the pronoun: He sees me, not he sees I, and we
have agreement between the third person subject and the verb. He sees,
not he see. We have also agreement between *this* and *that* and the
noun: these books, those books, and not this books and that books.
French also utilizes inflection in the pronominal forms: *Voici le livre de
Jeanne*; *je le lui donne*. The forms of the pronouns, *le, lui*, make clear
the antecedent to which they refer. There is agreement between the
noun and its modifying adjective and between the subject and the verb.

The use of agreement and inflection in both French and English have this in common: in both languages agreement and inflection are largely redundant. They are, in a sense, almost superfluous—the structural relationships are often sufficiently expressed by word order, and failure to express the accompanying agreement and inflection signals will be sensed as annoying mistakes by the native speaker, although they will seldom (may this be of some comfort to our students) interfere with the comprehensibility of the construction.

Finally, it is possible that structural relationships and meaning may be regulated by the words which we have referred to as function words, words which in themselves do not seem to carry lexical meaning, but which express relations or grammatical concepts. Such words are "future," "past," "possession of," as in I **have** left, I **will** go, the legs **of** the chair.

We can compare utterances in English and French which have the same structural meaning in both languages: statement, question, possession. If different media are used in the same type of utterance or if different media are used to convert one type of utterance to another, we may expect that the speaker of English will have trouble with the French utterance.

Let us give a few examples of uses of different media in French and English:

1. **French uses agreement, English does not.**

Vous lisez le journal.	You read the paper.
Nous lisons le journal.	We read the paper.
notre journal	our paper
nos journaux	our papers
le vieux livre	the old book
la vieille femme	the old woman

The fact that the above types of agreement between subject and verb or noun and modifiers are almost absent in English obviously causes many problems to the English speaker learning French.

2. **French uses inflection, English does not.**

Je la vois.	I see her.
Je lui donne le livre.	I give her the book.
Je le vois.	I see him.
Je lui donne le livre.	I give him the book.

The fact that French distinguishes a case system in the third person object pronoun, while English does not, is another source of errors for the student.

3. **English uses inflection, French uses function words.**

My brother's back   *Le dos de mon frère.*

This does not seem to cause any great trouble, perhaps because a construction paralleling French (for instance, the back of the book) exists also in English, and perhaps because it is generally easier to learn a function word construction instead of inflection than the reverse.

4. **English uses function words, French uses inflection.**

I'll read; I'm going to read.   *Je lirai.*

The problem here lies in the learning of the inflection form rather than in the difference of the media as such.

5. **English uses function words, French uses word order.**

Does he speak English?   *Parle-t-il anglais?*
Do we speak French?   *Parlons-nous français?*

Experience shows that there is comparatively little temptation for the American student to imitate the English function word construction in French. Interference from English exists only insofar as the French construction seems strange to the learner.

The most important interference caused by different media seems to occur when the student is not sufficiently aware of the medium being used; this is typically the case if intonation is used to change one pattern to another:

6. **Differences in the use of intonation patterns.**

The best example is the change from statement to question, which in French can be made by a change of intonation alone. In English a rising pitch replacing a falling pitch on the stressed syllable of a statement pattern would normally be used to express astonishment, in an echolike repetition of another person's statement:

A. Charles speaks ⌈French; B. Charles speaks French?

However, *Il parle français* with a falling pitch on the last syllable is a statement; with a rising pitch on the last syllable it is a question. Speakers of English are not only reluctant to use this simple question pattern in French, but they often misunderstand its use by a French speaker.

7. **English uses stress; French uses word order and/or function words.**

This is a very important category of interference caused by difference in media. We have already pointed out that stress is not phonemic in French. Thus, every difference produced in English by a variation of the stress pattern must have a different counterpart in French:

a ⌐French⌐ teacher   *Un professeur de français*
a French ⌐tea⌐cher   *Un professeur français*

Generally the English pattern of noun or gerund + noun must in French be expressed by a pattern of noun + preposition + noun or verb.

a gold watch   *une montre en or*
a sewing machine   *une machine à coudre*
a straw hat   *un chapeau de paille*

It is interesting to note here that the juxtaposition of nouns is now beginning to be accepted perhaps as a result of English influence, as in a service station, *une station service*.

The most obvious example of the use of stress in English is, of course, stress for the purpose of emphasis. In French the place of emphasis is generally the end of the ascending stress group, where the highest pitch occurs. Since this place of highest pitch is fixed by the pattern, French can stress an element of a sentence only by maneuvering it into the place of highest pitch, by rearranging the entire construction.

The following examples will illustrate those principles and demonstrate this basic difference between English and French.

(a) I am giving this book to Paul.   *Je donne ce livre à Paul.*

   I am giving this book to ⌐Paul.   *C'est à Paul que je donne ce livre.*
(b) Charles knows the truth.   *Charles sait la vérité.*
   Charles ⌐ knows the truth.   *C'est Charles qui sait la vérité.*
(c) This boy is intelligent.   *Ce garçon est intelligent.*
   That boy is in⌐tel⌐ligent.   *Il est intelligent, ce garçon-là.*
(d) I saw him today.   *Je l'ai vu aujourd'hui.*
   I saw him to⌐da⌐y.   *C'est aujourd'hui que je l'ai vu.*
(e) I like this boy.   *Ce garçon me plaît.*
   I ⌐ like ⌐ this boy.   *Il me plaît, ce garçon.*
(f) Your answer is a real surprise.   *Votre réponse est une vraie surprise.*
   Your answer is a ⌐ real sur⌐prise.   *C'est une vraie surprise que votre réponse.*

(g)   I don't know the answer.   *Je ne sais pas la réponse.*
      I don't know the answer. $\left\{\begin{array}{l}\textit{Moi, je ne sais pas la réponse.}\\ \textit{C'est moi qui ne sais pas la réponse.}\end{array}\right.$

This mechanism of emphasis is an important part of the French language and should be drilled in specific exercises. For instance, the student can be asked to emphasize the successive elements of an utterance. The teacher gives a sentence like *Robert aime ce tableau* and indicates to the student which elements are to be emphasized. This will elicit such responses as *C'est Robert qui aime ce tableau, Robert l'aime, ce tableau, C'est ce tableau que Robert aime.* Another possibility is to set up a pattern exercise—perhaps in question and answer form:

Teacher: Student:

Est-ce que ce garçon est intelligent?   *Oui, il est intelligent, ce garçon.*
Est-ce que cette jeune fille est belle?   *Oui, elle est belle, cette jeune fille.*
Est-ce que vous avez vu Charles hier?   *Oui, c'était hier que je l'ai vu.*

Est-ce que vous avez lu ce livre aujourd'hui?   *C'est aujourd'hui que je l'ai lu.*

Est-ce que vous avez rencontré Jeanne hier soir?   *Oui, c'était hier soir que je l'ai rencontrée.*

In another type of exercise the teacher may elicit the emphasis construction by asking questions for different parts of the same sentence. For instance, with the base sentence *Robert étudie son livre de français dans la classe d'anglais:*

Teacher: Student:

Qui étudie son livre de français?   *C'est Robert qui étudie son livre.*
Qu'est-ce que Robert étudie?   *C'est son livre de français que Robert étudie.*

Où Robert étudie-t-il son livre de français?   *C'est dans la classe d'anglais qu'il étudie son livre de français.*

Failure to use the emphasis mechanism of French is largely responsible for the lack of vividness and general impression of lifelessness created by the otherwise grammatically correct French of many students.

(C) THE MECHANISM OF INTERFERENCE:
PATTERN CONFUSIONS

The difference in media and the sheer necessity of learning new forms ,
and vocabulary are only partially responsible for the student's difficulties.
The difference in media is, as a matter of fact, not even one of the major
obstacles. The most difficult problem is, as pointed out in Chapter II,
that created by the student attempting to equate parts of French and
English constructions. But if the student can predict with absolute
certainty that French will always use an inflection whenever the English
uses a function word, his problem will then be merely to learn the specific
French form and there will be no further difficulty. A language in which
all media, although different, existed in a one-to-one correspondence
with the media of another language would be merely a coded form of
that other language. The most persistent problems faced by the student
are not those created by radical differences but by those due to a partial
similarity or overlap between the two languages, which the student
extends by analogy into an area in which the overlap does not exist.
An examination and analysis of mistakes made by hundreds of students
on French examinations at the University of Michigan showed that
actually only a small percentage (15%–20%) of all mistakes are due to
what one might call complete lack of learning, meaning that the student
simply did not know a French word or form. The vast majority of
mistakes (60%) were traceable to students having "learned" some
French–English correspondence which was then extended into an
area where it does not exist. As we have noted in Chapter III, language
study has a unique position among other subjects insofar as the most
frequent source of error, interference, is not due to absence of learning
but is built into the learning mechanism itself.

   In the following discussion we shall try to trace the most frequent
sources of errors caused by this parallelism and correspondence between
French and English. The categories we can establish are not absolutely
rigid. In some cases English may interfere with a particular French
construction for more than one reason, and assignment to one or the
other category has to take place on a somewhat arbitrary basis. Still,
we hope that our discussion and examples will cover the most important
cases of structural interference due to parallelism and correspondence.

   We may define as **parallel constructions** all those in which each
French element corresponds to an element in the English construction;
in both the French and English construction the corresponding elements

make the identical contribution to the total structural and lexical meaning of the utterance. For example, *Je* (1) *vois* (2) *le* (3) *garçon* (4) = I (1') see (2') the (3') boy (4'). Such constructions are hardly, if ever, missed by the student. But as we have pointed out before, this 1 = 1', 2 = 2', 3 = 3', 4 = 4' correspondence becomes the basis of errors elsewhere.

Types of Interference

1. **Parallel constructions with identical structural meaning exist in French and English; but these parallel constructions do not always correspond to the same lexical items.**

This category of conflict is a very difficult one to combat, since the student's native speech habits and the existence of the parallel construction in French conspire to force the students into errors:

Example (A):   **The use of different type of object structures by different verbs.**

English	*French*
I work for John. I speak for Charles.	*Je travaille pour Jean.* *Je parle pour Charles.*
I ask for Mary.	*Je demande Marie.*
I see Mary. I know Robert.	*Je vois Marie.* *Je connais Robert.*
I obey John.	*J'obéis à Jean.*
I speak to John. I write to John.	*Je parle à Jean.* *J'écris à Jean.*
I think of John.	*Je pense à Jean.*
I speak of Charles.	*Je parle de Charles.*

The problem illustrated above concerns, fortunately or unfortunately, some of the most frequently used verbs of French: *attendre* (to wait for), *regarder* (to look at), *chercher* (to look for), *cacher à* (to hide from), *payer* (to pay for). We say unfortunately because their frequent occurrence gives the American student many opportunities to make mistakes. It is, however, fortunate in that the very frequency of these constructions makes it comparatively easy to build such verbs into the practice material and patterns of any early French courses.

It seems advisable (1) to drill the construction of these verbs in exercises especially designed for that purpose, such as a substitution exercise using different objects in *je paie le livre*; (2) to use these verbs in connection with drilling other more complicated syntactical patterns, thus affording the student automatically the additional practice with object constructions. In other words, it is just as easy to use *attendre l'autobus* or *chercher le livre* as substitutions in a pattern drilling the use of the subjunctive as it would be to practice these patterns with *parler à Jean* or *trouver le stylo*, and it would be more profitable.

Example (B): **The connections between verbs and the dependent infinitives.**

English	French
I can study. I must study.	*Je peux étudier.* *Je dois étudier.*
I want to study.	*Je veux étudier.*
I begin to study. I continue to study.	*Je commence à étudier.* *Je continue à étudier.*
I decide to study.	*Je décide d'étudier.*
I go to Paris (in order) to study.	*Je vais à Paris pour étudier.*

Thus the construction with or without a function word before the infinitive exists both in French and in English. The situation is further complicated by the fact that French has three possible function words, *de, à, pour*, while English has only one, to.

Again we are faced with a frequently found construction and a type of error that can, by continuous repetition, become ingrained in the student's speech habits. The most frequent infinitive constructions such as: *je vous permets* (*défends, demande*) *de faire quelque chose: je réussis* (*commence, continue*) *à faire quelque chose: j'aime* (*espère, préfère, veux*) *faire quelque chose* should thus be drilled fairly early in any French course, probably best by substitution exercises in *Je vous défends de partir, je commence à étudier*, and so on. Special drill is necessary; a list of verbs requiring *de*, *à*, or nothing before the dependent infinitive, securely hidden away in the appendix of the textbook, cannot by itself solve the problem.

2.   **Parallel constructions exist in French and English; but the parallelism is broken by French alone.** Unlike the preceding category, the French construction which "breaks" the parallelism has no English counterparts.

Example (A):

English		French
He speaks of him	(Charles).	*Il parle de lui.*
He speaks of her	(Jeanne).	*Il parle d'elle.*
He speaks of it	(car).	*Il en parle.*
He speaks of it	(money).	*Il en parle.*

Example (B):

English	French
Is he sick?	*Est-il malade?*
Are we sick?	*Sommes-nous malades?*
Is Charles sick?	*Charles est-il malade?*

In the above examples the French grammatical principles should be pointed out to the student. The exercises for replacing nouns by pronouns (Example A) or making sentences interrogative (Example B) will take care of the required drill.

In some instances the parallelism with English is not broken according to a grammatical principle but rather by a definite number of lexical items. The idioms with *avoir* are a case in point:

Example (C): **"Idiomatic" expressions with *avoir*.**

English	French
I am sick. We are lazy.	*Je suis malade.* *Nous sommes paresseux.*
We are wrong. We are right. We are hungry.	*Nous avons tort.* *Nous avons raison.* *Nous avons faim.*

In a case like the above, the number of expressions breaking the parallelism must simply be learned and practiced. Learning grammatical rules is of little avail. If a conceptual or grammatical difference is involved, it must of course be explained—as for instance the break of parallelism presented by:

English	French
The coffee is hot. The sun is hot.	*Le café est chaud.* *Le soleil est chaud.*
Charles is hot.	*Charles a chaud.*
It is hot (today).	*Il fait chaud (aujourd'hui).*

In an example such as the preceding, the French pattern should be contrasted for the student and the difference in concept pointed out to him before he ventures into wrong analogical expressions like *Il est chaud* (= it is hot).

Example (D): **Verbs conjugated with *être*:**

English	French
He has seen Charles. He has found Charles.	*Il a vu Charles.* *Il a trouvé Charles.*
He has arrived. He has left. He has fallen. He has died.	*Il est arrivé.* *Il est parti.* *Il est tombé.* *Il est mort.*

The break in this parallel is at least partly predictable by grammatical rules: verbs conjugated with *être* are never followed by a direct object. In any case, the number of verbs conjugated with *être* is comparatively small and these verbs must simply be learned—not as a list to be memorized, but through exercises in which their *Passé Composé* is used in the context of complete sentences. The conjugation with *être* of reflexive verbs is a completely ironclad grammatical rule (it does not quite fit into the category under discussion since the reflexive verb construction of French does not parallel English in any case because of the position of the reflexive pronoun). At any rate, the shifting of constructions from the present to the *Passé Composé* is probably the best type of exercise for drilling conjugation with *être* as opposed to *avoir*.

Example (E):　**Nouns modified by the indefinite article**:

English	French
He is ┊ a good student.	*C'est* ┊ *un bon étudiant.*
He is ┊ a bad teacher.	*C'est* ┊ *un mauvais professeur.*
He is ┊ a teacher.	*Il est* ┊ *professeur.*

As long as the singular noun in French is modified by an adjective the noun construction after *être* parallels or at least corresponds to English. Both English and French use the indefinite article. But without a modifying adjective, French does not distinguish between noun and adjective after the verb *être*, as in *il est professeur, il est intelligent*. We note, incidentally, that the parallelism of "a good student" with *un bon étudiant* is broken if the expressions are shifted into the plural:

English	French
He is ┊ a good student.	*C'est* ┊ *un bon étudiant.*
She is ┊ a bad actress.	*C'est* ┊ *une mauvaise actrice.*
They are ┊ bad students.	*Ce sont* ┊ *de mauvais étudiants.*

This particular problem is best drilled in exercises contrasting the different French patterns. We may ask the student to shift sentences like *C'est un bon professeur* into the plural or we may go through a conversational response exercise: *Quelle est la profession de M. Smith? Il est professeur. Quelle sorte de professeur est M. Smith? C'est un bon professeur. Quelle est la profession de M. Dupont? Il est ingénieur. Quelle sorte d'ingénieur est M. Dupont? C'est un bon ingénieur.*

In some cases the parallelism with English exists only within a certain number of expressions; and in the majority of cases English and French patterns clash:

English	French
a good student a bad student a young student	*un bon étudiant* *un mauvais étudiant* *un jeune étudiant*
an intelligent student a lazy student	*un étudiant intelligent* *un étudiant paresseux*

The "normal" position of the French adjective is after the noun which it modifies, but a limited number of frequently used adjectives (*bon, mauvais, haut, gros, grand, beau, joli, autre, nouveau,* et cetera) are parallel to English. The situation is further complicated by the fact that some adjectives can be used with different meaning before and after the noun, as will be pointed out in the following chapter.

The position of adjectives in French must thus become the object of special exercises. Especially important are substitution exercises in which the student first places adjectives such as *paresseux, intelligent,* into a pattern like *C'est un étudiant americain* and is then asked to repeat the same exercise using *bon, mauvais, jeune,* et cetera. The final step is to use both categories of adjectives in the same exercise, making the student choose the correct position before or after the noun.

Example (F): **The position of the object pronoun.**

English	French
Give me the book! Find it! (the pen).	*Donnez-moi le livre.* *Trouvez-la!*
Don't give me the book. He gives me the book.	*Ne me donnez pas le livre.* *Il me donne le livre.*

In this example, too, the parallelism with English is established by a rather limited number of constructions. French uses the object pronoun after the verb only in a few instances: the affirmative imperative, the emphasis construction (*Il donne le livre à moi, pas à lui*), with *ne . . . que* (*Il ne donne le livre qu' à moi*), after a limited number of verbs like *penser, songer, être* (*Le livre est à moi, Il pense à moi*) and the comparatively rare cases in which the use of *me, te, se, nous, vous* as direct objects before the verb necessitates the use of *à* + stressed pronoun for the expression of the indirect object pronoun (*Il vous présente à moi*). Still, all these cases, especially the comparatively frequent imperative construction, establish a parallel with English. The object pronoun position must thus be taught in drills which contrast the use of the post-verbal stressed pronoun with that of the unstressed pronoun. For instance:

Est-ce qu'il vous explique le livre?	*Oui, il me l'explique.*
Est-ce qu'il explique le livre aussi à Robert?	*Non, il ne l'explique qu'à moi.*
Est-ce qu'il vous donne de l'argent?	*Oui, il m'en donne.*
Est-ce qu'il donne de l'argent aussi à Robert?	*Non, il n'en donne qu'à moi.*

Other types of drills may be used, shifting imperatives from the positive to the negative or contrasting the construction of *penser, songer,* et cetera, with that of other verbs in pronoun substitution exercises.

One point should be made clear in connection with the entire category of problems created by the break in parallelism between French and English. Experience has shown that *it is much easier to teach the contrasting constructions if the parallel ones are not introduced simultaneously but are presented only after the contrasting constructions have been firmly established.* This can easily be done in those cases shown in Examples (E) and (F), in which the parallel construction is less frequent. In other words, the fact that French adjectives follow the noun, or that French object pronouns precede the verb, should be drilled first so that they appear to the student as one to one correspondence. The student will then have comparatively little trouble with the position of the pronoun or the adjective. It is the existence of the parallel construction which sets the most persistent interference mechanism into motion. Students who have produced *il me donne le livre* quite easily and naturally will often come up with *il donne moi livre* only after they have been introduced to the affirmative imperative or the use of the stressed pronouns in expressions like *il pense à moi*.

3.   A pattern correspondence between English and French is broken by French.

This type of interference is probably the most common. After all, only a limited number of French constructions parallel English completely. The more general situation is that French and English constructions correspond under specific circumstances. The student, consciously or subconsciously, remembers this correspondence and applies it in another situation where it does not exist.

Example (A):   **The use of the partitive article and the use of the definite article for generalization.**

English	French
I am buying candy. I am selling candy.	*J'achète des bonbons.* *Je vends des bonbons.*
I like candy. I don't like candy.	*J'aime les bonbons.* *Je n'aime pas les bonbons.*
I am not buying candy. I don't eat too much candy.	*Je n'achete pas de bonbons.* *Je ne mange pas trop de bonbons.*

The situation is a very typical one: an English construction, the use of the noun without the article, has several corresponding constructions in French. There are two complementary ways of attacking the problem: (1) the mechanical one of drilling the students in the use of the partitive after certain verbs or expressions, while the use of the definite article construction is drilled after others; (2) the explanation of the difference in concept. The latter is undoubtedly necessary because the teaching of the partitive merely on the basis of vocabulary or structural clues will leave the student confused and puzzled about sentences like *j'aime beaucoup les bonbons* vs. *j'achète beaucoup de bonbons*, or *je n'aime pas les bonbons* vs. *je ne mange pas de bonbons*. Conceptual differences not expressed in English are not always clearly seen by the speaker of English. It is at this point that explanation, possibly reinforced by visual aids, must come into play. A simple picture contrasting the whole ◯ with a small part of it ▷ may help the student to realize that *L'or est un metal* or *j'aime les jeune filles* are statements generalizing about categories, whereas *je mange des pommes de terre* or *je suis sorti avec des jeunes filles* can apply only to an infinitesimal part of a whole category.

Example (B):   **Dependent infinitive construction vs. subordinate clause.**

English	French
I permit him to study. I forbid him to study.	*Je lui permets d'étudier.* *Je lui défends d'étudier.*
I want him to study.	*Je veux qu'il étudie.*

In the above case the break of correspondence does not seem easily explainable on the basis of a grammatical rule or concept, and the pattern with *vouloir* (mandatory use of the dependent clause) must be drilled as a special problem. For instance, we can make up a little story about a student's activities during a day: *Il étudie sa leçon; Il va au cinéma; Il boit de la bière; Il fume des cigarettes;* and ask the class to express whether or not his activities correspond to his parents' wishes: *Ils veulent qu'il étudie sa leçon. Ils lui permettent d'aller au cinéma. Ils ne veulent pas qu'il boive de la bière.*

Example (C):   **Future vs. present in a subordinate clause.**

English	French
I shall talk to him if he comes to London.	*Je lui parlerai s'il vient à Londres.*
I shall talk to him when he comes to London.	*Je lui parlerai quand il viendra à Londres.*

The problem created by the use of the future in the above example can be fairly easily explained in terms of the surrounding structure and can thus be drilled in terms of that structure (the student is asked to replace *si* by *quand, lorsque, après que,* and so on, to make the concomitant change of tense).

Example (D): **Indicative vs. subjunctive in a subordinate clause.**

English	French
I hope he will come tomorrow. I think he will come tomorrow. I know he will come tomorrow.	*J'espère qu'il viendra demain.* *Je crois qu'il viendra demain.* *Je sais qu'il viendra demain.*
I don't think he will come tomorrow.	*Je ne crois pas qu'il vienne demain.*

Again the break in correspondence can be accounted for by the clues given by the pattern itself. The subjunctive appears almost automatically after certain expressions used in the main clause: *penser* and *croire* in the negative, *douter, vouloir, exiger, permettre, défendre* and expressions of emotion (*se réjouir, avoir peur*) necessitate the use of the subjunctive in the subordinate clause that follows. There is no need here to review these various expressions and categories, which are to be found in any French grammar. The point is that these expressions must be taught as automatic clues for the use of the subjunctive in the subordinate clause. This does not mean that the student should not be made to grasp the meaning of the subjunctive: for instance, that it expresses an action which someone wants to have performed by some one else (*je veux que vous partiez*); an action the actuality of which is uncertain (*je doute qu'il ne vienne*); or an action in which the subject of the main clause is emotionally involved (*Robert se réjouit que vous soyez arrivé*). A grasp of the meaning of the subjunctive is especially useful in those few cases in which the surrounding structure does not furnish the automatic clue, and in which the use of the subjunctive carries a differentiation of meaning not expressed elsewhere in the construction: *Il parle à haute voix de sorte que nous puissions comprendre* vs. *Il parle à haute voix de sorte que nous pouvons comprendre*. In the first sentence our understanding is the intended result of speaking, loudly, and this is expressed by the subjunctive alone. *Vous connaissez un homme qui peut m'aider* is a statement of fact and the existence of the man who can help is taken for granted. *Vous connaissez un homme qui puisse m'aider?* is an inquiry. The existence of the man, and his being able to help, are doubtful. In this latter example the use of the subjunctive is really a concomitant change; we have to switch from statement to question. The student will have some difficulty understanding and using the construction unless he has a general idea of what the subjunctive implies.

The student's ability to use the subjunctive in conversation depends primarily on exercises in which its use is made automatic habit. Thus, drills on the use of the subjunctive might primarily consist of exercises in which the student replaces different kinds of main clauses *je crois que vous avez raison*: replace *je crois* by *je doute, je suis sûr, je ne crois pas, j'espère*) or different kinds of conjunctions *il est parti avant que Charles soit arrivé*; replace *avant que* by *après que, parce que, quoique*).

Special care should be taken that the exercises involving the choice of subjunctive versus indicative be taken up only after the subjunctive clues themselves have been thoroughly drilled. Some students are also apt to confuse the use of the subjunctive in object clauses (after the conjunction *que*, depending on the verb in the main clause) with the use of the subjunctive in adverbial clauses (where its use depends on the conjunction). They will want to use the subjunctive in the subordinate clause in a sentence like *je me réjouis parce qu'il sait la réponse* because of the clue furnished by *je me réjouis*. Thus special exercises may be needed contrasting the two types of uses of the subjunctive, for instance substitution exercises in which *que* and conjunctions like *parce que, quand*, are alternated in sentences like the example just given.

The category of multiple French correspondence to the same English construction is a rather large one. Examples could easily be multiplied. Before leaving the category, let us point out that the perennial problem of the use of the imperfect versus the *Passé Composé* belongs to this category. This problem is a good example for a case in which pattern drill and structural clues are of limited use: *Je suis allé au cinéma* and *J'allais au cinéma* are both correct French. The correct use of the one versus the other depends on a grasp of their meaning. In order to use the imperfect correctly the student must understand its nature as describing an habitual or incomplete action, just as he must realize that the *Passé Composé* describes an action which is considered as completed.

4.   Pattern correspondence between English and French is broken by English.

In some instances, the student's difficulty is evidently created by the fact that English is not consistent in its own pattern. The student is unlikely to see this lack of consistency in his native language and may be confused by the resulting break in French–English correspondence.

Example (A):   **English verbs not using the progressive tense.**

English	French
I have been studying French for two years. I have been reading for two hours.	*J'étudie le français depuis deux ans.* *Je lis depuis deux heures.*
I have been here for two days. I have known him for years. I have understood this since yesterday.	*Je suis ici depuis deux jours.* *Je le connais depuis des années.* *Je comprends cela depuis hier.*

In this case French will consistently use the present tense for an action begun in the past and continuing into the present. English uses the **perfect progressive** tense to convey the same meaning. But this correspondence is broken with those English verbs (be, know, like, see, need, understand, want) which are not usually used in a progressive form, and this peculiarity should be pointed out to him.

This problem also exists in the case of past action, as in I had been studying (= *j'étudiais*); but I had known this for two years (= *je savais . . .*).

Example (B):   *Passé Composé* **vs. Present.**

English	French
I have studied French in school. I have never been in Paris.	*J'ai étudié le français à l'école.* *Je n'ai jamais été à Paris.*
I have been in Paris for two days.	*Je suis à Paris depuis deux jours.*
I have been studying French for two years.	*J'étudie le français depuis deux ans.*

This is related to Example (A). Whereas a form like I have studied, or I have read will normally be expressed in French by the *Passé Composé*, with those English verbs which do not use the progressive form, the student must determine by the context whether to use the French Present or the *Passé Composé*.

Another nice English–French correspondence which is spoiled by those English verbs not using the -ing form is the one between the past progressive (I was reading) and the French imperfect (*je lisais*). With most verbs it is possible to tell the student that an imperfect must be used in French whenever the form was (were + ing) is used or can at least be implied or substituted in the English sentence corresponding to French. But with the verbs mentioned above the -ing form is not possible ("I knew," not "I was knowing," "I saw," not "I was seeing") and the student must again rely on his understanding of the concept.

5.   French seems to break the consistency of its own pattern.

Of course any example given in (3) above can be used here. The basic difference involved between this category and (3) is that the break in consistency does not necessarily involve a break in correspondence with English. In many cases the wrong construction used by the student as a result of his wrong extension of a French pattern will not in any way be caused by English interference; as a matter of fact, English interference should or could in some cases have produced the correct French form. The student who says *la plupart d'étudiants* or *la plus grande partie de lait* obviously makes his mistake under the influence of a French pattern such as *beaucoup d'étudiants, beaucoup de lait*. Such a mistake is, in a sense, a minor triumph of French over English interference—yet it is a mistake just the same.

Following are some examples of such breaks in French patterns, in which the inconsistency of French alone rather than any break in French–English parallelism seems to cause the main difficulty.

Example (A):   **The position of *personne* vs. *rien*, *pas*, et cetera, in compound tenses.**

Je n'ai rien vu. *Je n'ai pas vu.* *Je n'ai jamais vu.*
Je n'ai vu personne.

The last sentence in the example is often missed by the student in spite the position of anybody in English: I did not see anybody. At the same time the mistake of misplacing *rien* under the influence of English I did not do anything also occurs. This can be drilled by asking the student to transform sentences such as *je ne vois rien*, or *je ne vois personne* into the *Passé Composé*.

Example (B):   **The position of adverbs with compound tenses.**

J'ai	déjà	parlé à Charles.	
J'ai	souvent	parlé à Charles.	
J'ai		parlé à Charles.	hier.
J'ai		parlé à Charles	d'ailleurs.

French has two patterns for the position of adverbs in compound tenses. Some adverbs, such as *déjà, souvent, toujours,* are placed before the past participle, while most other adverbs cannot appear between the auxiliary and the past participle, and usually stand at the end of the sentence. The situation is further complicated by the fact that some English adverbs (the "frequency" words like always, occasionally, often, sometimes, rarely, never) follow the pattern of *déjà, souvent, toujours,* while most other English adverbs are placed at the end of the sentence. At any rate, the possible adverb positions in French must be contrasted with each other. This can be done best in substitution exercises in which the student puts words like *déjà, toujours, d'ailleurs, autrefois,* into sentences like *J'ai lu ce livre, Nous avons parlé à Robert.*

Example (C):   **Use of pronouns with *penser, songer, rêver* and *être*.**

Le professeur	obéit	à sa femme.	Il	lui	obéit.	
Le professeur	parle	à sa femme.	Il	lui	parle.	
Le professeur	pense	à sa femme.	Il		pense	à elle.
Le professeur	songe	à sa femme.	Il		songe	à elle.

This contrast may be drilled by having students use the pronoun form in answers to questions like:

Est-ce que vous parlez	à Robert?	Oui, je lui	parle.
Est-ce que vous obéissez	à Charles?	Oui, je lui	obéis.
Est-ce que vous pensez	à Charles?	Oui, je	pense à lui.

Example (D):   **The use of the noun after *ni*, without the determinative.**

Je	mange			du	pain.		
Je	mange			des	saucissons.		
Je ne	mange	ni			pain	ni	saucissons.

Here the use of the noun without the article after *ni* corresponds to the English usage but is often missed by the student because of the change in the French pattern. This change can be drilled in exercises in which the student responds negatively to the following type of questions:

Voulez-vous du thé?	*Non, je ne veux*	*pas de*	*thé.*
Voulez-vous du café?	*Non, je ne veux*	*pas de*	*café.*
Voulez-vous du café	*Non, je ne veux ni*		*café ni thé.*
ou du thé?			

Example (E):   **The use of the noun inversion for the formation of the interrogative.**

Quand	arrive	Charles?	
Que	fait	Charles?	
Comment	va	Charles?	
Pourquoi		Charles	vient-il?
Qui		Charles	regarde-t-il?
Quand		Charles	est-il arrivé?

The possibility of forming the interrogative by inverting the noun exists only in certain cases: after the interrogative adverbs *quand, comment, où, combien* (but not after others) after the pronoun *que* (but normally not after *qui*), and not with compound verbs or in sentences in which the verb is further modified. This pattern conflict is likely to confuse the student. Pedagogically, it is certainly preferable not to introduce the conflicting question patterns such as *est-ce que*, noun inversion, inversion with pronouns simultaneously, but rather successively, after each one of the patterns has been thoroughly drilled and firmly established. These patterns can then be contrasted in exercises in which the student is directed to form questions corresponding to:

Robert arrive	*à midi.*	=		*Quand*	*arrive*	*Robert?*
Robert fait	*son devoir.*	=		*Que*	*fait*	*Robert?*
Robert voit	*Marie.*	=		*Qui*		*Robert voit-il?*
Robert est arrivé avec	*son ami.*	=	*Avec*	*qui*		*Robert est-il arrivé?*

6. Two French patterns are confused by the students.

Practically all the interference patterns discussed so far may, of course, be due to confusion of the French pattern. What is meant here is a somewhat more specific confusion, obviously not involving any interference from English or any break of consistency within French, but the possibility of the student's confusing two or more basically quite unrelated French constructions. Perhaps the best example of this kind of interference is the partitive after *pas*, which is confused by the student with the negative construction of a verb requiring the preposition *de*:

Positive	Negative	
Je bois de la crème.	*Je ne bois pas de*	*crème*
Je bois de la bière.	*Je ne bois pas de*	*bière.*
Je parle de la leçon.	*Je ne parle pas de la*	*leçon.*

Many students will miss the negative construction of the third sentence above because they think of *pas de* as a structure required under any and all circumstances.

A similar confusion of French pattern is likely to occur because of the contrast between the negative of the partitive and that of the construction of *de* + noun after the verb *être*, used for identification:

Positive	Negative
Je mange du pain.	Je ne mange pas de pain.
Nous sommes des ennemis. C'est du lait.	Nous ne sommes pas des ennemis. Ce n'est pas du lait.

The partitive becomes *de* after the negative, but *des, du, de la* of the "identification construction" after the verb *être* remains the same. Again the student may easily be misled and use *de* after *pas* under the influence of the partitive. In all cases like the above, the shift occurring within French must be contrasted in pattern drills, structural signals (such as not using *pas de* after *être*) pointed out and the difference in construction explained to the student.

7.   An English construction type has no counterpart in French.

There are many English constructions which cause interference in corresponding French patterns simply because the student transposes the English construction literally into French: the mechanism of a break in parallelism or even correspondence do not appear to be involved.

Example (A):   **The indirect object marked by word order in English.**

> I give Charles the book.
> *Je donne le livre à Charles.*

In French it is impossible to indicate the direct and the indirect object of the verb by word order. (Note that the interference caused by the above construction appears also if the indirect object is a pronoun: I give him the book. Many American students will fail to distinguish *lui* and *le* in the equivalent French sentence).

Example (B):   **Passive construction with following direct object.**

> Charles was given the book.
> *On a donné le livre à Charles.*
> (*Ce livre a été donne à Charles.*)

In English the indirect object of a verb can become the subject of a passive type sentence: They told me the story > I was told the story by them; and, I was allowed to do this, I was ordered to do that. In French only the direct object of the active construction can conceivably become the subject of a passive sentence: *Charles a donné le livre à*

Robert: only *le livre* is eligible to become the subject of a passive sentence.

Example (C):   **Relative clause without relative pronouns.**

> The man you talked to ...
> *L'homme à qui vous avez parlé ...*
> The man you saw ...
> *L'homme que vous avez vu ...*

The possibility of forming a clause modifying a noun without a relative pronoun does not exist in French.

Example (D):   **Word order in relative clauses or questions beginning with "whose."**

> The man whose daughter you know ...
> *L'homme dont vous connaissez la fille ...*
> Whose son is he?
> *De qui est-il le fils?*

Note that English puts the object modified by whose at the beginning of the sentence while French does not change the word order of **subject-verb-direct object**. The situation here is further complicated by the break in consistency within the French pattern: *l'homme dont je connais le fils* vs. *l'homme au fils de qui je viens de parler.* The latter contrast creates interference of the type described previously in category 5.

Example (E):   **Impossibility of separating unstressed pronouns from verb.**

> I always come late.   *Je viens toujours en retard.*
> He often drinks coffee.   *Il boit souvent du café.*

In French, no adverb may be placed between the unstressed subject pronoun and the verb. This conflicts with the English pattern of placing adverbs of frequency before the verb. In French the only words which may be placed in this position are other unstressed pronouns or other verb satellites.

This category (7) offers many examples. Let us mention a few of the most important English constructions which are *per se* a menace to accuracy in French: a friend of mine, I am studying (or any English progressive tense); three of them (or any other construction with of + pronoun following a pronoun or adjective as in all of us, none of them, some of us); something (someone) new; I continue studying (or any other verb form ending in -ing used as noun, such as swimming is a sport); I wash my hands; I had the student repeat the sentence;

He who speaks; The one who came; Did they arrive in time? No, they didn't (or any negative or interrogative pattern using do); how fast, how much, how long, very much, et cetera. There is no need for us to give here the correct French equivalents, nor the faulty word-to-word translations into French which are—*hélas!*—only too familiar to the French teacher. The question is what to do about them. Evidently the corresponding French constructions must be made the subject of special drills. Since the problem does not involve any pattern conflict within French, the best type of exercise to be used is the substitution drill. Overt comparison of the French construction with the English counterpart may often be helpful. The author of this book has quite successfully used the device of writing constructions like "a friend of mine" on the blackboard and crossing them out, thus warning the student against literal translation. Yet while such a device tells the student what not to do, the positive remedy must always be with the active practice of the French pattern.

8. **French uses different function words or replacement words (pronouns) corresponding to the same English replacement of function word.**

In this kind of interference the problem is created by multiple word correspondence, rather than syntactical patterns alone. Since the words involved are pronouns which have no independent lexical meaning and function words expressing structural meaning rather than lexical meaning, we mention this category in our discussion of syntax. Actually the differentiation between function word and lexical word is not a precise one and the category of interference to be discussed here overlaps partly what will be treated in the following chapter on vocabulary problems.

In this category there seem to be two distinct possibilities: either the function word to be used depends on a lexical item in the structure, or it depends entirely on the structure itself. Example A will illustrate both possibilities:

Example (A): *De or à following an adjective introducing a dependent infinitive.*

English	French
I am ready **to** leave.	*Je suis prêt **à** partir.*
I am happy **to** leave.	*Je suis content **de** partir.*

In the above example the use of *à* vs. *de* depends on the preceding adjective used in the construction. It is in no way dependent on the construction itself and correct usage should be established by substitution exercises which force the student to use different adjectives (*heureux de, lent à*) in the above construction.

This type of alternative in the use of a function word is rare. Usually the choice between one function word and another depends on a structural clue which can be explained to the student. The construction of *il est difficile d'étudier le français* vs. *le français est difficile à étudier* is a case in point. In the construction, impersonal *il* + *est* + adjective, the latter is followed by *de*; whereas in the construction, noun (pronoun) + *est* + adjective *à* must be used if the noun or pronoun beginning the construction is really the object of the action of the infinitive.

> *La porte est difficile à ouvrir.*
> *Le professeur est impossible à comprendre.*

Thus the two types of construction can be contrasted in pattern drills:

Est-il facile de faire ce devoir?   *Oui, ce devoir est facile à faire.*
Est-il impossible de comprendre la   *Oui, la leçon est impossible à*
leçon?   *comprendre.*

Example (B): **French function words corresponding to English "what."**

English	French
What is happening?	*Qu'est-ce qui se passe?*
What are you doing?	*Qu'est-ce que vous faites?*
What are you thinking of?	*A quoi pensez-vous?*
What is geometry?	*Qu'est-ce que c'est que la géométrie?*
What a noise!	*Quel bruit!*
I know **what** is happening.	*Je sais ce qui se passe.*
I know **what** he is doing.	*Je sais ce qu'il fait.*
I know **what** he needs.	*Je sais ce dont il a besoin.*
What is your suggestion?	*Quelle est votre suggestion?*

The above sentences underline essentially one point discussed earlier in this book: the student must learn **complete structures**. The only solution to the learning of function words is simply to learn them not as "words" but as part of the structure in which they occur. The structures themselves can, of course, be contrasted in suitable pattern exercises. For example:

TEACHER: STUDENT:

Qu'est-ce qu'il fait?   Je ne sais pas ce qu'il fait.
Qu'est-ce qu'il en pense?   Je ne sais pas ce qu'il en pense.
De quoi a-t-il peur?   Je ne sais pas ce dont il a peur.

Example (C): **Conjunction vs. preposition.**

English	French
I know this **because of** his illness.	Je sais cela **à cause de** sa maladie.
I know this **because** he is ill.	Je sais cela **parce qu'il** est malade.
I knew this **before** his departure.	Je savais cela **avant** son départ.
I knew this **before** he left.	Je savais cela **avant qu'il** soit parti.

English generally uses the same function words before a noun construction as before a dependent clause, while French does not. The resulting confusion on the part of the student learning French can be avoided if the contrasting French constructions are pointed out to him. The pattern practice involved in the necessary drill should consist of substitution exercises in which the student is asked to replace *avant que* by *avant, après que* by *après, sans que* by *sans, parce que* by *à cause de,* or vice versa and to make necessary additional changes. There are numerous instances of the conflicts between French and English created by French using two or more function words or pronouns corresponding to the same English word. We shall conclude our discussion of syntax by enumerating some of the most important cases without giving detailed examples.

(D)   The entire set of problems created by French having two sets of personal pronouns, one used only as satellite of the verb cluster (the

conjunctive pronouns), and another set that can actually take the syntactical position of a noun cluster (the **disjunctive** pronouns).

(E) The differences between French relative pronouns and interrogative pronouns, (*l'homme que vous voyez* and *qui voyez-vous?*: *qui, que,* = English whom).

(F) The use of *personne, quelqu'un, n'importe qui*, all of which can be associated with English "anybody" by the student, just as *rien, quelque chose, n'importe quoi* may become identified with "anything." It can be pointed out to the student that *personne* and *rien* are negative words ordinarily used only in negative sentences while *quelqu'un* and *quelque chose* are used only in positive or interrogative but not in negative sentences. *N'importe qui* or *n'importe quoi*, on the other hand, correspond to a heavily stressed English "anybody" or "anything" equivalent to "anybody" or "anything at all!"

(G) The use of *plus* vs. *davantage*, the latter being used only if the comparison is not completed.

Charles travaille plus que Robert. Jean travaille encore davantage.

Rather than give examples, let us conclude our discussion of such interference by quoting a sentence once produced by a Freshman in his first semester's examination: *Je sais cela que garçon sait ce* (I know that that boy knows that)—an impressive testimony for the necessity of learning function words as part of structures.

One point should be stressed again most emphatically. Our discussion is based primarily on English and French comparison, because English interference is the enemy the teacher is constantly fighting. We must know the exact nature of the psychological and linguistic mechanism which may cause the student's errors. But all of this does not mean that overt comparison between English and French is necessarily the best way of fighting the enemy. Just how much direct comparison between the two languages should take place depends on various circumstances. The author's view is that in the beginning course such overt comparison should be brief and be restricted to the interference discussed under types 4 and 7 above. It can be used more freely in review courses for remedial purposes. It is of prime importance in active phases of advanced composition and translation. In the beginning courses it is probably more advisable to use pattern contrasts within French as a teaching tool even though the underlying problem may be at least partly due to English interference. The danger of using the method of comparing English and French is obvious; the student, instead of using French patterns freely and without reference to English, may become confused by the discussion of English–French differences and comparisons. The understanding of the nature of interference is necessary equipment for the teacher, but not necessarily for the student. For the latter it can in no way substitute for the drill and actual use of the French speech patterns themselves.

CHAPTER IX

Teaching Vocabulary

The teaching of vocabulary deals with the learning of the forms and meanings of words, those semantic units which, in spite of the lack of a clearcut linguistic definition, seem to present concepts which are quite evident to everyone. We have already mentioned that function words which signify relationships and grammatical meanings belong properly to the realm of structure or syntax. In addition there are other word groups we can exclude from consideration in teaching vocabulary: first of all pronouns, which in a sense have no independent meaning of their own. Secondly, there are words whose use depends very largely on grammatical considerations; the exact use of words like some, any, neither, more, and their counterparts in French such as *pas, rien, plus, davantage*, is more of a grammatical than a lexical problem. They were discussed in our consideration of syntax rather than vocabulary, for the correct usage of these words depends primarily on learning them within a structure. For example, the use of *de* in an expression like *je suis content de son arrivée*, or the use of *aux* in *une jeune fille aux cheveux roux* must be learned as part of the total construction and it does not seem advisable to teach such words as lexical items.

In this chapter, then, we shall discuss the problem of teaching those words which we may call **content** words, words on which the lexical part of the meaning of a sentence depends: the nouns, verbs, adverbs, and adjectives, which are the lexical "meat" of the utterance.

Again, just as in the discussion of syntax, we note a great degree of parallelism and overlap between English and French. Again we can say that this parallelism is a blessing as well as a curse and that we must

155

consider it from both points of view. Let us first look at the possible disadvantages of overlap and parallelism by outlining the major categories of interference connected with the learning of lexical meanings.

(A) INTERFERENCE MECHANISM IN LEARNING VOCABULARY

We have stated that the difference between function words and vocabulary (lexical) words is difficult to define. The same difficulty in separating precisely and categorically structural and lexical factors applies also to the cause of interference in the learning of vocabulary items. The typical cause of interference is the same as in the interference with structures: a partial overlap in one area is wrongly extended into another. The student learns *il est arrivé à temps* (in time), and on the basis of an equation, time = *temps* forms a sentence like *Je l'ai vu trois temps*. In practically all the categories of interference mentioned below, the basic problem is the identification of an English word or concept with a French word or concept on a simple one-to-one basis. In our discussion of types of interference we shall start with those in which the causes of difficulty are due to structural problems and then go on to the discussion of those in which the underlying problem is primarily one of distinguishing different concepts.

1. **Interference caused by difference in structural use.**

A good example for this category is the problem experienced by many students in finding the French counterparts of *better* or *worse*, *best* or *worst*. The problem is really structural rather than lexical: English does not distinguish the adjectival from the adverbial use, but French does: *mieux* vs. *meilleur*, *pis* vs. *pire*, et cetera. The solution to the problem is to establish for the student the distinction between adverbial and adjectival use with adverbs and adjectives which are distinguished in English, enabling students to make the distinction between their French counterparts with ease. For example:

La réponse de Charles est plus correcte.	*Il répond plus correctement que Jean.*
La réponse de Charles est plus intelligente.	*Il répond plus intelligemment que Jean.*

After the student has understood the grammatical pattern of the above sentences, we point out in which of the above frames *mieux* and *meilleur* belong and we drill the student on the correct substitutions—*La réponse de Charles est meilleure, Il répond mieux que Jean.*

2. Lexical meaning expressed through a structure different from the structural type used in English.

In this category the problem is not overlap in lexical meaning but the type of construction used. The lexical meanings involved in *Je viens de faire mon travail, je me rappelle mon devoir, je me souviens de ma promesse, j'ai envoyé chercher le médecin,* are clear and do not conflict with English lexical meanings. The only problem is the French construction. Since we are dealing with a structural problem, the solution lies in pattern drill; for example, we might ask for substitution in a sentence like *Il a envoyé chercher le médecin.* Expressions like *entendre dire que* and *entendre parler de* belong to this category. The concept involved is clearly the one that corresponds closely to English hear. The problem is again the construction. We can ask the student to substitute nouns or clauses in a phrase like:

J'ai entendu parler de ses idées.

Substitute:

qu'il est intelligent	*J'ai entendu dire qu'il est intelligent.*
son oncle	*J'ai entendu parler de son oncle.*
qu'elle est belle	*J'ai entendu dire qu'elle est belle.*
ses suggestions	*J'ai entendu parler de ses suggestions.*

Thus leading him to make the concomitant changes from *dire que* to *parler de.*

3. Different French lexical items corresponding to the same English items in different structures or contexts.

In this category again the difficulty is caused not so much by overlapping lexical meaning as by similar or identical lexical meanings expressed by different words in different structures. English say, tell, speak, all have meanings basically similar to French *dire, raconter, parler.* The fact that it is not possible to establish a one-to-one correspondence between any of these will cause considerable difficulty to the student. These English and French words cut up, so to speak, the same semantic area but they do it somewhat differently. The use of *dire* vs. *parler* vs. *raconter* must be learned through the use in context and especially through the observation of whatever structural clues are available: *dire* is used before a subordinate clause or a dependent infinitive or a noun (*Il m'a dit que vous avez raison; Il m'a dit de rester, Il m'a dit la vérité*); *parler* is not used in such a context. It may be followed by *de* + noun (*Parlez-moi d'amour*), while *dire* is not followed by that type of construction. Whatever conceptual differences there are must also be exploited and fully explained. For example: (*Il m'a dit de venir*) *dire* may be used with the meaning of "command, order" whereas *raconter* cannot be used in such a context.

4. Different lexical items corresponding to the same English item (the conceptual difference is clear to the English speaker).

This category does not present a very great problem. Since the different concepts involved are clear to the English speaker, he is usually quite willing to accept the different French equivalents: "I left the room" and "I left my book in the room" correspond to *Je suis sorti de la chambre* and *J'ai laissé mon livre dans la chambre*. The difference between the two kinds of "leaving" is fairly obvious and, if necessary, can be made even clearer by simple illustration. In connection with this we can also point out the distinction between *partir de*, *sortir de*, and *quitter* (with obligatory direct object), which involves not only a structural difficulty but a somewhat more subtle differentiation between types of "leaving" which can, however, be explained easily by a diagram or picture. The diagram below illustrates that *sortir de* implies "getting out" of a location. The dotted lines indicate the optional nature of the object with *sortir* and *partir*.

sortir de | *partir* | *quitter*

Various English two-part verbs (verb + preposition combinations such as make up, make out, get up, get on, get off, call up, call on) also belong in the category under discussion. Since English uses the same verb with so many different meanings one would expect that speakers of English might confuse the French equivalent or corresponding expressions. In fact, their usual trouble is simply that of not knowing the French equivalents rather than confusing them. Evidently the conceptual differences between expressions such as get and get up, or get on, are far too obvious to an English speaker for him to be led to use a word that he associates with get, in the meaning of get on or get up.

5. **Different lexical items corresponding to the same item in English (but the conceptual differences between French items are not obvious to the English speaker).**

This category, as one might expect, is one of the most difficult to deal with. Let us recall that this type of interference may also occur in the realm of structure. It may occur quite frequently in the category of "grammatically determined" words such as the use of *en* and *dans* as in *je l'ai fait en deux heures* (the time it took to finish) and *je le ferai dans deux heures* (the time that will elapse before it is done). Examples for it in the realm of lexical meaning proper are the usage of *jour, soir, matin, an* vs. *journée, soirée, matinée, année*; the use of *savoir* vs. *connaître*. Various attacks may be used. Since the problem is difficult they should be combined rather than used as alternates. We must search for whatever automatic structural clues there are. For example, we can point out to the student that *jour, matin*, and *an*, are used after the cardinal numbers while *journée, matinée, année*, are used after the ordinal numbers (*j'étudie le français depuis deux ans*: *c'est ma deuxième année de français*). We can point out that only *savoir* and never *connaître* may appear before a subordinate clause. These types of structural clues can be made the object of pattern practice (substitute *le professeur, où il travaille, mon oncle, la vérité*, in the frame *je connais M. Smith* and make the concomitant choice between *connais* and *sais*). This will help to narrow the possible area in which mistakes may be made purely because of confusion of concept. But the choice of *savoir* vs. *connaître* or *jour* vs. *journée* is not in all cases determined by the surrounding structure alone. The conceptual difference must then be explained, either simply by discussion in English and/or by the use of visual aids showing that *jour* is the measuring unit of time while *journée* is the duration of an action. A great deal of pedagogical work remains to be done in this particular area, to which structural linguistics, because of its preoccupation with the purely formal clues and ways of expressions, cannot contribute.

The category we have just discussed is a rather broad one and various other types of vocabulary interference belong to it. For instance, the variation of meaning which French may produce by using the same adjective either before or after the noun belongs here: *le dernier mois* vs. *le mois dernier*; *ce pauvre homme* vs. *cet homme pauvre*; *une nouvelle idée* vs. *une idée nouvelle*, are examples of French making a conceptual difference normally not expressed by English last, poor, new. These conceptual differences must be explained and illustrated (*le mois dernier* =

"past" vs. *le dernier mois* = "last of a series"). Pattern practice asking the student to place such adjectives before or after the noun would be an entirely meaningless procedure. To this category also belong many French and English words having basically similar lexical meanings; but the French word may, because of a particular context or particular use in a special region or social stratum, have a connotation not matched by the English counterpart. Again, explanation and warning may be necessary in order to have the student avoid the possible error or *gaffe*.

6. The *faux amis*.

So far we have discussed interference due to a partial overlap in meaning. There is also interference due to partial overlap in form—the *faux amis* or false cognates. By these we mean, in the pedagogical (not linguistic) sense, any English and French words which have a great resemblance in terms of orthography or sound but which have different meanings. Many textbooks contain lists of these *faux amis*, so that we need not give numerous examples here: Fr. *lecture*/Eng. lecture, Fr. *assister*/Eng. assist, Fr. *conférence*/Eng. conference, Fr. *attendre*/Eng. attend, Fr. *demander*/Eng. demand. Partial overlap in form can also be accompanied by a partial overlap in meaning: Fr. *initier* and Eng. initiate correspond in many instances, but the French word is normally not used in the sense of "taking the initiative," which is rendered by *entreprendre*, or *mettre en train*. Likewise *embarrasser* will correspond to embarrass in many instances but *est-ce que ce chapeau vous embarrasse?* means "Does this hat bother you" (in the sense of inconveniencing, not embarrassing). As a matter of fact, the more closely we watch the exact connotation and nuance, the more the concept of the "real friend" becomes vague, and the dividing line between *vrais amis* and *faux amis* is one of degree, since there is never absolute overlap in the usage of different words of different languages. There is rather a progression from *vrais amis* (almost complete overlap) to *faux amis* (no overlap at all).

A speaker of English trying to communicate in French will almost automatically put heavy reliance on the English–French vocabulary correspondences. The most obvious and common of the *faux amis* must therefore be pointed out and contrasted with the real French counterparts of the English words. The problem is not solved by a list in the appendix of the textbook, but by specific exercises. Perhaps the best way to bring the *faux amis* into focus is to use them in context next to each other, as in *Est-ce que Charles est allé à la bibliothèque? Non, il n'a pas besoin d'y aller puisqu'il a acheté ce livre à la librairie,* or *Qu'est-ce que Charles a fait quand il a fini la lecture de ce livre? Il est allé à la conférence de M. Dupont,* or *Pourquoi est-ce que Charles n'a pas pu assister à ce concert? Parce que son ami Jean ne l'avait pas aidé à faire son devoir.*

7. French interference

Just as in the realm of structure, there are some instances in which the primary source of the student's difficulty is not a lack of consistency between English–French correspondence, but rather a confusion arising from within the French system itself. The most obvious example is the confusion of similarity surrounding lexical items. The student may confuse *très* and *trop* merely because they look and sound partially alike. Aside from interference coming from English, the student may also confuse *le parti, la partie, la part* simply because of their partial resemblance in French. In order to avoid this kind of interference, similar expressions must be contrasted in context: *faire part* must be contrasted with *faire partie* in such a way that the difference becomes clear to the student: *Il m'a fait part de ses idées* (= *il m'a informé de ses idées*), *il ne faisait pas partie de mes amis* (= *il n'appartenait pas au nombre de mes amis*). Just as in the example, it is often advantageous to explain the similar French expressions in terms of synonymous structures. For purpose of drill the student may be given the synonym and be asked to express the equivalent ideas using either of the French constructions resembling each other, for instance use *faire part* and *faire parti* to express the meaning of sentences such as *Charles m'a informé de ses plans, Charles n'est pas un de mes amis.*

8. Idioms

The last example brings us to the general problem of idiomatic expressions. From the linguistic viewpoint the very idea of idiomatic expression is in need of clarification: we can, of course, call any expression or structure or vocabulary usage in which French and English are not parallel "idiomatic." From the linguistic point of view this definition, in which features of one language are defined in terms of the peculiarities of another, would be meaningless. From the purely pedagogical point of view it would not be too useful either. We have already noted that absolute parallelism between English and French rarely appears with complete consistency in the realm of structure. From the viewpoint of English, 75% of French is idiomatic. A meaningful linguistic approach to the concept of idiom must be based on French criteria alone. Simplifying the problem somewhat, we may suggest that we should call an "idiom" any form whose meaning cannot be deduced from the meaning of its components. *Porte-chapeaux*, (although it does not correspond to its English counterpart, hatrack) is not an idiom because its meaning is deducible from its components. But the construction *il y a* is an idiom, since its meaning is not clearly deducible from that of each of its components. Therefore its meaning must be learned like a vocabulary unit. In the realm of teaching vocabulary and lexical meaning we must be on the lookout for all expressions which have a total meaning in no way predictable from the meaning of the component parts: *attendre quelqu'un* (waiting for someone), even *avoir soif* (to be thirsty) are structural problems from the viewpoint of English, but to call them "idioms" does not seem to be useful. Real idioms, we suggest here, are such expressions as *se douter de quelque chose, en vouloir à quelqu'un, s'attendre à quelque chose, tout à l'heure, tout le monde*. They must be learned as units and their meaning must be contrasted with that of their individual components.

(B) TEACHING OF COGNATES

So far we have considered English and French similarities and overlaps only as a problem. There is, of course, little doubt that the existence of cognates (words similar in form and meaning in both languages) is also a great help which must be exploited to the fullest. In the teaching of cognates, two situations should be distinguished: teaching them as "active vocabulary" and teaching them for recognition purposes such as passive reading vocabulary. In the first situation they are likely to constitute a special pronunciation problem. The similarity in form intensifies English interference with the possibility of English reaction to French orthographic symbols; for instance, the reflex /ʃən/ instead of /sjɔ̃/ in words ending in -*tion* or -*sion* as in *communication, extension*. In either situation it is helpful to point out to the student the general pattern of cognate correspondence, but it is only in the passive reading situation that the student should be encouraged to rely on that pattern alone. Cognates taught for active use should be taught in connected speech patterns and in active production and the student should be warned against the active use of any cognate that has not been expressly presented in the vocabulary materials. The pattern of correspondence between French and English words to be presented here allow the student who is reading French to deduce the meaning of French words within a context. They are not predictors which enable the student to make up his own cognates for active use.

In many cases the French words and English words are orthographically identical or differ only in minor spelling patterns, which do not create any problems in identifying the French cognates, such as Eng. mortal/Fr. *mortel*, Eng. example/Fr. *exemple*, Eng. responsible/Fr. *responsable*. It may also facilitate recognition of certain cognates to point out to the student that the circumflex has generally speaking two functions: to differentiate two otherwise identically spelled words such as *sur* and *sûr*, *dû* and *du*; and to indicate that an *s* following that vowel was dropped as in *forêt, bête, fête, conquête, pâte*.

Some of the more important cognate patterns (omitting all those which are orthographically identical) of the realm of noun or adjective endings are:

English	*French*	
-or	-eur	professor-*professeur*
-ity	-ité	brutality-*brutalité*
-ary	-aire	commentary-*commentaire*
-y	-ie	academy-*académie*
-er	-re	chamber-*chambre*
-ous	-eux	dangerous-*dangereux*

In case of verbs there are also several distinct possible patterns. If we compare French infinitives with the English infinitives we find that perhaps the most frequent pattern is that a French infinitive ending corresponds to lack of any special verb ending in English, as in admit-*admettre*, desert-*déserter*, serve-*servir*. Most common corresponding verb ending morphemes in the infinitive are:

English	*French*	
-y	-ier	defy-*défier*
		study-*étudier*
-ish	-ir	punish-*punir*
		banish-*banir*
-ive	-oir	deceive-*décevoir*
		receive-*recevoir*
-(u)te	-(u)er	substitute-*substituer*
		constitute-*constituer*

-ate	-er	agitate-*agiter*
		meditate-*méditer*
-ize	-iser	normalize-*normaliser*
		realize-*réaliser*
-duce	-duire	produce-*produire*
		deduce-*déduire*
-duct	-duire	conduct-*conduire*
		deduct-*déduire*

Some cognate correspondences occur also in prefixes:

English	*French*	
de-, dis-	*dé-, dés-*	disorder-*désordre*
		denounce-*dénoncer*
es-, ex-	*é-*	escape-*échapper*
		exchange-*échanger*
s + consonant	*es-*	spirit-*esprit*
		stomach-*estomac*

The recognition and learning of the pattern of cognates of English and French are really a special application of the process we referred to at the end of the chapter on morphology: the learning of the derivational morphemes. In some cases the main root of the words as well as the derivational morphemes are cognates, as in stupidity-*stupidité*, and in others the derivational morpheme may not be a cognate of English although the root of the word is. At any rate, the recognition of the derivational suffix or prefix and separation from the stem will usually reveal the cognate. For example, once we know that *-esse* is a noun ending we can recognize the cognate and with it the total meaning of *délicatesse*, *sagesse*, et cetera. Once we recognize the prefix *mé(s)* as a derivational prefix, indicating "negation" or "contrary to" we can make an informed guess at the meaning of *mécontent*, and *mésaventure*.

(C) GENERAL PROBLEMS IN TEACHING VOCABULARY

The main contribution which linguistics can make to the teaching of vocabulary lies in those aspects which have been discussed under (A) and (B) above: the comparison between English and French vocabulary and the process of derivation. There are many other aspects of the teaching of vocabulary, less directly connected with linguistics, which are nevertheless important. We shall mention them briefly. First of all there is the perennial problem of what words to teach, the problem of determining which words are the most frequent and thus most necessary. This problem has often been obscured by the failure to differentiate between function words, grammatically determined words and replacement words on one hand and content words on the other. The former are comparatively few in number, and are a necessary and inevitable part of the utterance. From the point of view of active production they must be taught as part of the structure; from the point of view of passive recognition they hardly need be taught at all. Their frequency of occurrence is so great that they teach themselves. As far as the content words are concerned, their frequency depends entirely on circumstances, and so does the necessity of knowing them. If someone wants to say something about the gearshift of a car, he needs to know the proper word; whether the word is "frequent" or not is quite irrelevant at that particular moment. Many of the frequency lists which have been established are based on works of literature—often heavily weighted with 19th Century novels. To use them as guides for the construction of teaching materials makes sense only insofar as it is our aim to prepare the student to read 19th Century French literature. If it is not, then this type of frequency list is of comparatively little use.

Another possible approach taken to vocabulary frequency is the one used in the construction of Basic English and the French methods based on the same general principle ("French through Pictures," et cetera). There the words included in the course are not those which are determined by a frequency count but those judged absolutely necessary to express essential concepts, and those which in turn can be used to express other concepts. The goal is the greatest possible economy. Hence all possible synonyms are avoided, as are vocabulary items which can be adequately expressed in other terms.

A third possible approach to frequency is the one taken in the development of *Le Français Fondamental* (see Bibliography: Vocabulary). This is a study of essential French, subsidized by the French government originally in order to determine the minimum amount of French that would have to be taught to inhabitants of the French colonies. Here again efforts are made to avoid duplication; but the overall approach is radically different from that of Basic English, since the words included in *Le Français Fondamental* are not those determined as important according to an artificially constructed list of essential concepts, but those which have been observed as the most frequent and necessary expressions of actual French speech. The French of the *Français Élémentaire* is thus "real" French, not a French that has been subjected to an artificial simplification for pedagogical purpose. Therefore it includes, quite necessarily, most of the essential function words and constructions of the French language. Learning the words and constructions of the *Français Élémentaire*, early in the French courses, should enable the student to communicate easily and naturally in the shortest possible time. The content words included in this system are objectionable only because it is impossible to determine the frequency and usefulness of such words from any absolute point of view.

An overall method for teaching vocabulary has been a subject of controversy and discussion for years. We have already indicated our views concerning the approach to vocabulary problems. As far as the overall method is concerned, linguistics is opposed to the teaching of English–French equivalents out of context, since such teaching will lead us not only to structural fragmentation but also to the student's making serious and often ridiculous errors in the use of vocabulary. In general a vocabulary item should never be learned without putting it into the context of an utterance. Of course, at times the student will be forced to use a dictionary, but if he consults the dictionary when reading French, the context will be provided by the passage. On the other hand, if he consults it for the purpose of forming a French sentence himself, a situation which should arise only in the more advanced stages of instruction, he must be trained to pay special attention to the sample sentences and contexts provided in the dictionary. Dictionaries which do not provide concise examples of the usage of words are obviously less than useless for composition or translation work.

Other methods of presenting vocabulary include explanation in English, explanation or definition in French (for example, *un paresseux est un homme qui ne veut pas travailler*), the use of synonyms or a series of synonyms (*vite = rapidement*), or the use of words with opposite meaning (*"paresseux" est le contraire de "diligent"*). The last three methods used have the obvious advantage of staying within French. They do have certain disadvantages. The French explanation may often be unclear and synonyms and antonyms cannot always be defined with perfect clarity and precision. Yet they seem preferable to explanation or giving the equivalent in English. In a French to French association, both members of the association (*clameur = bruit*; *jeune ↔ vieux*) are useful. In an English–French association, one of the members is, from the French teacher's viewpoint, quite useless. As we have pointed out in Chapter IV, the use of English seems indicated only if the French explanation becomes confusing or uneconomical.

Not only in this matter of frequency but also in the problem of overall method, much confusion arises because of failure to distinguish function words and grammatically determined words from content words. The former operate as part of, or are closely tied to, structure. To learn them correctly is primarily a matter of habit formation and automatic response reinforced by the understanding of grammatical structure. The content words, on the other hand, refer to specific concepts and objects in specific situations. They must be learned in association with such specific situations. It is, therefore, in the realm of vocabulary building that organization according to situations or "units of experience" seems particularly appropriate.

CHAPTER X

Conclusion: The Cultural and Literary Context

The necessity of learning at least lexical meaning in a definite situational context brings up an important problem: What kind of context? At what stage should the context include literature, or "cultural" material? These questions have been dealt with and discussed at length in many other publications. They are tremendously important questions, but because they are beyond the realm of linguistics we shall attempt only very brief answers. Culture, in the sense in which it is used by most linguists or cultural anthropologists, is the entire complex pattern of behavior and material achievements which are produced, learned, and shared by the members of a community. Language is part of culture, perhaps its most central part because it is largely language that makes the learning and sharing of behavior possible. Being the central part of culture, it is probably also the best key to that culture. Since it operates within a culture, it should be learned within contexts and situations which are part of that culture. Some cultural anthropologists—some of them linguists—have tried to analyze the cultural pattern of society in a way that corresponds closely to the structural analysis of the linguistic patterns. These cultural patterns (for example, the structure of family life, child rearing, attitude toward parents, children, and so on, and basic similarities in points of view which reappear in different forms in all of those areas) should ultimately become apparent to the student of the foreign language. Those patterns of French culture which clash with American patterns should receive special attention. Not only is the understanding of French the key to the understanding of French culture, but the reverse is also true. So far we have distinguished the lexical and the structural levels of meaning; but within a specific context there is also the cultural level. Unless we understand the cultural situation in which an utterance is made, we may miss its full implication or meaning. The tie of language study with culture is not an option to be discussed in terms of the preferences of the individual teacher, but actually a practical necessity. A student who reads about a Frenchman going to a *pharmacie* and pictures him going to an American drugstore is not getting the full meaning of what he is reading. A student who reads about a Frenchman cursing and equates the effect of his words with that which they might produce in an American milieu does not grasp the cultural meaning level of the situation.

Linguists have usually tried to associate elementary language study with culture in the anthropological sense, rather than with "culture" in the sense in which it is used when we mean the great artistic or literary achievements of a civilization. In some cases this may simply be due to the linguists' association with departments of anthropology rather than with departments of literature. There seems, nevertheless, to be some valid reason for connecting language instruction with anthropological culture rather than "culture" (and Literature), at least at the beginning level. The very understanding of literary works often depends on the grasp of the cultural environment in which their plots, characters, and themes operate. Of course, it is quite possible to approach culture through the literary work. Nor do we want to question the judicious use of literary works or the value of the learning or memorization of poetry in elementary courses. But we must keep in mind that the facets of culture presented in a literary work may be atypical, and particular care must be taken to choose literary works which will produce a real understanding of culture rather than an erroneous impression. And what is said about the teaching of culture applies even more to the realm of language: the language of the literary work is apt to be atypical. Many literature scholars and linguists believe that the very essence of literature may be defined by its use of special structure and vocabulary (this is obviously the case in poetry), and the very possibility of appreciating a literary work depends very often on recognizing the departures it makes from the structure and vocabulary of normal, everyday speech patterns. Only after we learn standard French can we really appreciate the individual particularly in the style of a Proust, a Camus, a Gide.

Bibliography

This bibliography does not claim to be exhaustive. It attempts to list a series of books which may serve as useful outside reading and which present in greater detail some of the material dealt with in this book. The asterisks used with the titles listed are an indication of their level of difficulty, and the degree of technical knowledge they either presuppose or attempt to impart. Books which do not presuppose a technical knowledge of linguistics and which do not aim at imparting a technical knowledge beyond the minimum needed for the application of linguistics in the classroom are not marked with asterisks. Others are preceded by either one or two asterisks: the two asterisks are reserved for the most technical works, of importance only to the reader with special interest in linguistics. The symbol (R) after a reference indicates that it is particularly recommended. Typically, the books marked with (R) are the ones that either contain documentation or additional reading supplementing individual chapters of the text.

Theoretical Foundations (General Linguistics, Phonetics, Psychology)

**BACH, EMMON. *An Introduction to Transformational Grammar.* New York: Holt, Rinehart and Winston, Inc., 1964.

*BLOCH, BERNARD, and TRAGER, GEORGE. *Outline of Linguistic Analysis.* Baltimore: Linguistic Society of America, 1942 (reprinted in 1950).

*BLOOMFIELD, LEONARD. *Language.* New York: Holt and Co., 1945.

CARROLL, JOHN B. *The Study of Language.* Cambridge, Mass.: Harvard University Press, 1953. (R).

———. "Research on Teaching Foreign Languages" in GAGE, NATHANIEL L., *Handbook of Research on Teaching.* Chicago: Rand McNally Co., 1963.

**CHOMSKY, NOAM. *Syntactic Structures.* Leyden: Mouton and Co., 1957.

*EISENSON, JON. *The Psychology of Speech.* New York: Crofts, 1946.

FERGUSON, CHARLES E. (Supervisor). *Teaching a Second Language* (Series of 5 films on 1. Nature of Language, 2. The Sounds of Language, 3. Organization of Language, 4. Words and Their Meanings, 5. Modern Techniques in Language Teaching), Teaching Manual to accompany film. Washington, D.C.: Center for Applied Linguistics, 1963. New York: Teaching Film Custodians, 1963.

*GLEASON, H. A., JR. *An Introduction to Descriptive Linguistics*. Revised Edition. New York: Holt, Rinehart and Winston, 1961.

HALL, ROBERT A., JR. *Linguistics and Your Language*. New York: Doubleday and Company, 1960.

**HARRIS, ZELLIG S. *Structural Linguistics*. Chicago: University of Chicago Press, Phoenix Books, 1963.

*HAAS, WILLIAM, UITTI, KARL D., and WELLS, RULON. *Linguistics*. Englewood Cliffs, N.J.: Prentice-Hall, Inc., 1964.

*HEFFNER, R. M. S. *General Phonetics*. Madison, Wis: University of Wisconsin Press, 1949.

*HILL, ARCHIBALD A. *Introduction to Linguistic Structures*. New York: Harcourt Brace and Co., 1958.

*HOCKETT, CHARLES F. *A Course in Modern Linguistics*. New York: The MacMillan Co., 1958.

HOIJER, HARRY, Editor. *Language and Culture* (Conference on the Interrelations of Language and other Aspects of Culture). Chicago: University of Chicago Press, 1954.

The Principles of the International Phonetic Association, Being a Description of the International Phonetic Alphabet and the Manner of Using It. London: International Phonetic Association, 1953.

*MARTINET, ANDRÉ. *La Description phonologique*. Paris–Génève: Société de publications romanes et françaises, Librarie Droz, M. J. Minard, 1956.

———. *Eléments de linguistique générale*. Paris: Collection Armand Colin, 1960.

**OGDEN, C. K., and RICHARDS, I. A. *The Meaning of Meaning*. New York: Harcourt Brace and Co., 1923.

*OSGOOD, CHARLES, and SEBEOK, THOMAS, Editors. *Psycholinguistics, a Survey of Theory and Research Problems*. Baltimore: Supplement to *International Journal of American Linguistics*, Waverley Press, 1954.

**PIKE, KENNETH. *Language in Relation to a Unified Theory of the Structure of Human Behavior*. Glendale, Calif.: Summer Institute of Linguistics, Part I, 1954; Part II, 1955; Part III, 1960.

**———. *Phonemics: A Technique of Reducing Languages to Writing*. Ann Arbor, Mich.: University of Michigan Press, 1947.

*———. *Phonetics: A Critical Analysis of Phonetic Theory and a Technique for the Practical Description of Sounds*. Ann Arbor, Mich.: University of Michigan Press, 1943.

*POTTER, SIMEON. *Modern Linguistics*. New York: W. W. Norton and Co., 1964.

RIVERS, WILGA M. *The Psychologist and the Foreign-Language Teacher*. Chicago: The University of Chicago Press, 1964. (R)

SAPIR, EDWARD. *Language: An Introduction to the Study of Speech.* New York: Harcourt Brace and Co., 1921 (Paperback edition: Harvest Books).

*SAPORTA, SOL, Editor. *Psycholinguistics: A Book of Readings.* New York: Holt, Rinehart and Winston, 1961.

*SAUSSURE, FERDINAND DE. *Cours de linguistique générale.* Publié par Charles Bally et Albert Sechehaye avec la collaboration d'Albert Riedlinger, Paris: Payot, 1955.

*————. *Course in General Linguistics.* Translated by WADE BASKIN. New York: Philosophical Library, 1959.

*SKINNER, B. F. *Verbal Behavior.* New York: Appleton-Century-Crofts, 1957.

*WEINREICH, URIEL. *Languages in Contact.* New York: Publications of the Linguistic Circle of New York, No. 1, 1953.

*WHATMOUGH, JOSHUA. *Language, a Modern Synthesis.* London: Secker and Warburg, 1956 (Paperback, Mentor Books, The New American Library, New York, 1957).

Applied Linguistics

ALLEN, HAROLD B. *Readings in Applied English Linguistics.* New York: Appleton-Century-Crofts, Inc., 1958.

BELASCO, SIMON, Editor. *Anthology for Use with a Guide for Teachers in NDEA Language Institutes.* Boston: D. C. Heath and Co., 1961.

*BLOOMFIELD, LEONARD. *Outline Guide for the Practical Study of Foreign Languages.* Baltimore: Linguistic Society of America, 1942.

CORNELIUS, EDWIN T., JR. *Language Teaching (A Guide for Teachers of Foreign Languages).* New York: Thomas Crowell Co., 1953.

FRIES, CHARLES C. *Teaching and Learning English as a Foreign Language.* Ann Arbor, Mich.: University of Michigan Press, 1945.

LADO, ROBERT. *Linguistics Across Cultures, Applied Linguistics for Language Teachers.* Ann Arbor, Mich., University of Michigan Press, 1957. (R)

————. *Language Teaching: A Scientific Approach.* New York: McGraw-Hill Book Co., 1964. (R)

MARTY, FERNAND. *Linguistics Applied to the Beginning French Course.* Roanoke: Audio-Visual Publications, 1963. (R)

VALDMAN, ALBERT, and BELASCO, SIMON, Editors. *Applied Linguistics, French. A Guide for Teachers.* Boston: D. C. Heath and Co., 1961. (R)

General Methodology, Classroom and Laboratory Techniques

"What do we know about Teaching Modern Foreign Languages?," *Audio Visual Instruction,* Vol. 4, No. 6 (September, 1959) (National Education Association, Department of Audio-Visual Instruction).
Entire volume is devoted to language instruction, laboratory equipment and techniques. See also Vol. 7, No. 9 (November, 1962).

BROOKS, NELSON. *Language and Language Learning, Theory and Practice, Second Edition.* New York, Harcourt, Brace and World, 1964. (R)

French for Secondary Schools. Albany: New York State Education Department, 1960. (R)

CAPRETZ, PIERRE J. (Project Director). *Audio Lingual Techniques for Teaching Foreign Languages* (includes a 60-minute film on the teaching of French). Washington, D.C.: Norwood Films, 1963.

CHILDERS, J. WESLEY, *Foreign Language Teaching*. New York: The Center for Applied Research in Education, Inc., 1964.

COCHRAN, ANNE. *Modern Methods of Teaching English as a Foreign Language: a guide to modern materials with particular reference to the Far East*. Washington, D.C.: Educational Service, 1954. (R)

Foreign Languages, grades 7–12, Curriculum Bulletin Series, No. 5, tentative. Hartford, Connecticut: State Department of Education, 1958.

COUNCIL OF CHIEF STATE SCHOOL OFFICERS. *Purchase Guide (for programs in science, mathematics, foreign languages)*. Boston: Ginn and Co., 1959.

FINN, JAMES D., and PERRIN, DONALD G. *Teaching Machines and Programed Learning, A Survey of the Industry—1962*. Washington, D.C.: U.S. Department of Health, Education and Welfare, Office of Education, OE-34019, 1962.

HIRSCH, RUTH. *Audio-Visual Aids in Language Teaching (Monograph Series on Languages and Linguistics*, No. 5. Washington, D.C.: The Institute of Language and Linguistics, Georgetown University, 1954.

HOCKING, ELTON. *Language Laboratory and Language Learning*. Washington, D.C.: Department of Audio-Visual Instruction, National Education Association, 1964. (R).

HUEBENER, THEODORE. *How to Teach Foreign Languages Effectively*. New York: New York University Press, 1959.

———. *Audio-Visual Techniques in Teaching Foreign Languages, a Practical Handbook*. New York: New York University Press, 1960.

HUTCHINSON, JOSEPH C. *Modern Foreign Languages in High School: The Language Laboratory*. Washington, D.C.: Office of Education, 1961.

IODICE, DON R. *Guidelines to Language Teaching in Classroom and Laboratory*. Washington, D.C.: Electronic Teaching Laboratories, 1961.

JESPERSON, OTTO. *How to Teach a Foreign Language*. New York: The MacMillan Co., 1904.

JOHNSTON, MARJORIE C., and SEERLEY, CATHERINE C. *Foreign Language Laboratories in Schools and Colleges*. Washington, D.C.: U.S. Department of Health, Education and Welfare, Bulletin 1959, No. 3, 1959.

KONE, ELLIOT H., Editor. *Language Laboratories—Modern Techniques in Teaching Foreign Languages*. New York: Bulletin of the Connecticut Audio-Visual Education Association, Vol. 19, 1959–60.

LADO, ROBERT. *Language Testing*. The Construction and Use of Foreign Language Tests, a Teacher's Book. London: Longmans Green and Co. Ltd., 1961. (R)

LEON, P. R. *Laboratoire de langues et correction phonétique, Essai méthodologique*. Paris: Didier, 1962.

MARTY, FERNAND L. *Language Laboratory Learning*. Wellesley, Massachusetts: Audio-Visual Publications, 1960. (R)

———. *Programming a Basic Foreign Language Course: Prospects for Self-Instruction*. Hollins, Virginia: Audio-Visual Publications, 1962.

MÉRAS, EDMOND A. *A Language Teacher's Guide, Second Edition.* New York: Harper and Bros., 1962. (R)

MORTON, R. "The Language Laboratory as a Teaching Machine," *International Journal of American Linguistics* XXVI (1960), 113–166.

NEWMARK, MAXIM, Editor. *Twentieth Century Modern Language Teaching.* New York: Philosophical Library, 1948.

NOSTRAND, HOWARD LEE *et al. Research on Language Teaching: an Annotated International Bibliography for 1945–1961.* Seattle: University of Washington Press, 1962

O'CONNOR, PATRICIA. *Modern Foreign Languages in High School: Pre-reading Instruction.* Washington, D.C.: OE-2700, Bulletin 1960, No. 9. (R)

OLLMAN, J., Editor. *Selective List of Materials.* New York: Modern Language Association, 1962. (R)

O'ROURKE, EVERETT V. *et al. French, Listening, Speaking, Reading, Writing.* Sacramento: California State Department of Education, 1962. (R)

PLEASANTS, JEANNE VARNEY *et al. Audio-Visual Aids and Techniques in the Teaching of Foreign Languages.* A Report of the Committee on Teaching Aids and Techniques of the 1955 Northeast Conference on the Teaching of Foreign Languages, 1956.

STACK, EDWARD M. *The Language Laboratory and Modern Language Teaching.* New York: Oxford University Press, 1960. (R)

WALSH, DONALD D. *What's What. A List of Useful Terms for the Teacher of Modern Languages.* New York: The Modern Language Association of America, 1963.

WATTS, GEORGE B. "The Teaching of French in the United States: A History," *French Review,* Vol. XXXVII (1963), No. 1.

French Phonetics, Teaching of French Phonetics

*ARMSTRONG, LILIAN EVELINE. *The Phonetics of French.* London: G. Bell and Sons Ltd., 1947.

BURROUGHS, ELIANE. *A Programed Course in French Phonetics* (Palo Alto: Encyclopedia Britannica Films, 1961).

CAPON, A. J. E. *Avec ou sans liaisons, A Guide to Present-day Usage for Students of French.* Oxford: Basil Blackwell, 1963.

*COUNTENOBLE, H. H. *Studies in French Intonation.* Cambridge, England: W. Heffer and Sons Ltd., 1934.

DENKINGER, MARC. *Essentials of French Pronunciation.* Ann Arbor, Mich.: George Wahr Publishing Co., 1952. (R)

DELATTRE, PIERRE. *Les difficultés phonétiques du français.* Middlebury, Vermont: Ecole française, Middlebury College, 1948. (R)

———. *Principes de phonétique française à l'usage des étudiants anglo-américains.* Middlebury, Ecole française d'été, Middlebury College, 2nd ed., 1951. (R)

**FOUCHÉ, PIERRE. *Traité de prononciation française.* Paris: Librairie C. Klincksieck, 1956.

GENEVRIER, P. *Précis de phonétique comparée française et anglaise.* Paris: Didier, 1927.

GRAMMONT, MAURICE. *Traité pratique de prononciation française*. Paris: Delagrave, 1954.

GUITARD, LUCIEN, and MARANDET, LÉON. *French Phonetics*. Cambridge, England: Cambridge University Press, 1959.

MERCIER, LOUIS JOSEPH ALEXANDRE. *French Pronunciation and Diction, with a Special Study of American Speech Habits*. New York: Silver, Burdett and Co., 1929.

NICHOLSON, GEORGE GIBB. *A Practical Introduction to French Phonetics for the Use of English Speaking Students and Teachers*. London: MacMillan and Co., 1927.

ORR, JOHN. *Words and Sounds in English and French*. Oxford: Blackwell, 1953.

PLEASANTS, JEANNE VARNEY. *Phonetic French Dictionary* (with records). New York: Goldsmith's Music Shop, Inc., 1959. (R)

———. *Prononciation française—Intonations—Morceaux Choisis* (records). New York: Goldsmith's Music Shop, Inc., 1958. (R)

TILLY, EDMUND. *Aid to French Pronunciation with numerous drawings and exercises for use in schools and colleges*. New York: MacMillan and Co., 1925.

VALDMAN, ALBERT, SALAZAR, ROBERT, and CHARBONNEAUX, MARIE-ANTOINETTE. *A Drillbook of French Pronunciation*. New York: Harper and Row, 1964.

VARNEY, JEANNE VIDON (see PLEASANTS). *Pronunciation of French* (Articulation and Intonation). First Experimental Edition, Third Reprint, 1945.

General Works on French Structure (Morphology, Syntax)

*BOER, CORNELIS DE. *Syntaxe du français moderne*. Leiden: Universitaire Pers, IIᵉ d., entièrement revue, 1954.

BRUNOT, FERDINAND. *La Pensée et la langue; méthode, principes et plan d'une théorie nouvelle du langage appliqué au français*. Paris: Masson et Cie., 1922.

CLARK, RICHARD E., and POSTON, LAWRENCE, JR. *French Syntax List: A Statistical Study of Grammatical Usage in Contemporary French Prose on the Basis of Range and Frequency*. New York: H. Holt and Co., 1943.

*DAMOURETTE, JACQUES et PICHON, EDOUARD. *Des Mots à la pensée; essai de grammaire de la langue française*. Paris: Collection des Linguistes contemporains, 5 Vols., 1911–30.

DAUZAT, ALBERT. *Le Guide de bon usage; les mots, les formes grammaticales, la syntaxe*. Paris: Librairie Delagrave, 1954.

———. *Grammaire raisonnée de la langue française*. Lyon: Collection des langues du monde, 1947.

GOUGENHEIM, GEORGES. *Système grammatical de la langue française*. Paris: Bibliothèque du français moderne, J. L. L. d'Artrey, A. Rontely—d'Artrey, 1938.

GRÉVISSE, M. *Le Bon Usage* (7th edition). Paris: Duculot, 1961.

**HALL, ROBERT A., JR. *Structural Sketches I, French*. Baltimore: Waverley Press, Linguistic Society of America, Language Monograph No. 24, 1948.

IMBS, PAUL. *L'Emploi des temps verbaux en français moderne; Essai de grammaire descriptive*. Paris: C. Klincksieck, 1960.

MUELLER, THEODORE, and MAYER, EDGAR. *Structure of French.* Detroit: Wayne State University Press, 1962. (R)

VINAY, J. P. et DARBELNET, J. *Stylistique comparée du français et de l'anglais: méthode de traduction.* Paris: Didier, 1958.

WAGNER, R. L., and PINCHON, J. *Grammaire du français classique et moderne.* Paris: Hachette, 1962.

*WARTBURG, WALTER VON, and ZUMTHOR, PAUL. *Précis de syntaxe du français contemporain.* Bern: A. Francke, IIe éd., entièrement remaniée, 1958.

French Vocabulary (Synonyms, Cognates, Frequency)

ANSCOMBRE, J. *Synonymes et homonymes français.* Paris: Collection "J'apprends seul," n.d. Free copies offered by La Maison des Instituteurs, 13 Boulevard Victor Hugo, St-Germain-en-Laye (S-O).

Le Français Fondamental. Philadelphia, Pa.: Chilton Books, 1959.

CHEYDLEUR, FREDERIC D. *French Idiom List* (based on a running count of 1,183,000 words). New York: Publications of the American and Canadian Committee on Modern Languages, Vol. 16, 1929.

FAURRÉ, PIERRE. *Premier Dictionnaire en images; Les 1300 Mots fondamentaux du français.* Paris: Didier, 1957.

FREI, HENRI. *Le Livre de deux mille phrases.* Genève: Droz, Société de publications romanes et françaises, No. 40, 1953.

GOUGENHEIM, GEORGES. *Dictionnaire fondamentale de la langue française.* Paris: Didier, 1958.

GOUGENHEIM, G., RIVENC, P., MICHÉA, R., and SAUVAGEOT, A. *L'Elaboration du français élémentaire—étude sur l'établissement d'un vocabulaire et d'une grammaire de base.* Paris: Didier, 1956.

HENMON, V. A. C. *A French Word Book Based on a Count of 400,000 Running Words.* Madison: University of Wisconsin, Bureau of Educational Research, Bulletin No. 3, 1924.

KOESSLER, MAXIME, and DEROCQUIGNY, JULES. *Les Faux Amis (ou les trahisons du vocabulaire anglais).* Paris: Librairie Vuibert, 1928.

LACROIX, U. *Les Mots et les idées, dictionnaire des termes cadrant avec les idées.* Paris: F. Nathan, 1956.

Petit Larousse. Paris: Librairie Larousse, 1959. (R)

MAQUET, CHARLES. *Dictionnaire analogique; répertoire moderne des mots par les idées, des idées par les mots.* Paris: Larousse, 1937.

RAT, MAURICE. *Dictionnaire des locutions françaises.* Paris: Larousse, 1957.

SEWARD, ROBERT D. *Dictionary of French Cognates.* New York: S. F. Vanni, n.d.

VANDERBEKE, GEORGE E. *French Word Book.* New York: The MacMillan Co., 1939.

French Textbooks

The books included in the following list illustrate specific pedagogical devices discussed in this book. They show some impact of linguistic orientation. The statements accompanying the titles below indicate the chief reasons for including each book and the features it illustrates. These statements are not meant to be complete evaluations of the textbooks mentioned.

BART, BENJAMIN F. *La France, Carrefour des Civilisations.* New York: Harcourt, Brace and Co., 1949.
This book contains an introductory section applying morphological derivation to the study of vocabulary and English–French cognates.

BAUER, CAMILLE. *La France Actuelle.* Boston: Houghton Mifflin Co., 1963.
A second year college cultural reader which contains an adaptation of the reading material to spoken French and pattern drills.

BAUER, CAMILLE, BARTON, MARGARET, and O'CONNOR, PATRICIA. *Le Français: lire, parler et écrire.* New York: Holt, Rinehart and Winston, Inc., 1964.
The third in the series of the Holt, Rinehart, Winston materials. Aims are improvement of reading skills and composition while maintaining audio-lingual practice.

BENAMOU, MICHEL, and CARDUNER, JEAN. *Le Moulin à paroles (Méthode avancée de composition et de conversation).* Boston: Ginn and Co., 1963.
Application of audio-lingual pattern practice techniques on the advanced level.

BRUNSVICK, YVES, and GINESTIER, PAUL. *De la Langue à la civilisation française.* Paris: Didier, 1957–62.
Series of works (*Vers la France, A Paris, En France, Entrons dans la vie française*) based on the *Français élémentaire* study, utilizing pictorial aids, direct method, two color (red, black) print to emphasize grammatical principles.

BORGLUM, GEORGE, SALVAN, JACQUES, and MUELLER, THEODORE. *Images de France.* Detroit: Audio-Visual Materials Consultation Bureau, Wayne State University, 1956.
Each lesson contains a presentation of cultural materials in which each sentence is tied with the presentation of picture slides; pattern practice of the transformation and substitution type.

COTÉ, DOMINIQUE G., LEVY, SYLVIA NARINS, and O'CONNOR, PATRICIA. *Le Français: Ecouter et Parler.* New York: Holt, Rinehart and Winston, 1962.
The first in a series of a complete program for six years for Junior High through High School. The basic methodology is the audio-lingual approach, structural recombination of elements first learned in conversations, and pattern practice. Teacher's edition, Teacher's manual, workbook, flash cards, tapes, et cetera, are available.

DECKER, HENRY W., and BERNARD, FRANÇOISE. *Modern French: First Course.* New York: American Book Co., 1962. *Modern French: Intermediate.* New York: American Book Company, 1963.

Both books rely heavily on pattern practice techniques and "over-learning" of habitual responses.

DESBERG, DAN, and KENAN, LUCETTE ROLLET. *Modern French.* New York: Harcourt, Brace and World, Inc., 1964.
First year college text centered around conversations, supplemented by pronunciation and pattern drills. Records, tapes and teachers' manual are available.

DOSTERT, LÉON. *Français, Premier Cours.* Milwaukee: Bruce Publishing Co., 1958.
An attempt to combine a fairly traditional presentation of grammar with pedagogical devices such as pattern practice, primarily of the substitution variety. English to French translation is sometimes used as a pattern practice device, and French orthography, phonetic transcription and English translation are used next to each other in the introductory lessons.

DOSTERT, LÉON, and LINDENFELD, JACQUELINE. *Français, Cours Moyen, Civilisation.* Milwaukee: Bruce Publishing Co., 1963.
Continuation of *Premier Cours.* Grammatical principles are derived from narrative type selections.

EBACHER, JOSEPH P. *Atala by François-René de Chateaubriand.* Englewood Cliffs, N.J.: Prentice-Hall Inc., 1964.
The first in a series of readers utilizing the method devised by J. P. Ebacher: by interlinear annotation of content words for the first five times of their occurrence, the method eliminates "looking up in the dictionary" and calls attention to essential structure.

Correlated Language Tapes. Washington, D.C.: Electronic Teaching Laboratories, 1963.
Pattern drills using minimal vocabulary. A booklet correlating these drills with several well known textbooks is available.

French A (a film). Wilmette, Ill.: Encyclopedia Britannica Films, Inc., 1962.
First part of an elementary French course for the High School level.

EVANS, JAMES A., and BALDWIN, MARIE. *Learning French the Modern Way* (Book 1 and Book 2). New York: McGraw-Hill Book Co., Inc., 1963.
Texts for the first two levels of High School instruction which are integrated with tapes, film strips, motion pictures, teachers' manuals, tests. The material centers around conversations which are utilized for pattern drills. Third and fourth level materials are in preparation.

HAGIWARA, MICHIO P., and POLITZER, ROBERT L. *Continuons à parler.* New York: Blaisdell Publishing Company, 1965. Pronunciation exercises, auditory comprehension and structure drills for the intermediate course.

HARRIS, JULIAN, and LÉVÊQUE, ANDRÉ. *Basic Conversational French, Third Edition.* New York: Holt, Rinehart and Winston, 1962.
Grammatical principles, questions, pattern drills are derived from basic conversations on various subjects of cultural interest.

HOPE, QUENTIN. *Spoken French in Review.* New York: The MacMillan Co., 1963. Lessons based on literary materials, contain audio-lingual, pattern practice drills.

LANGELLIER, ALICE, LEVY, SYLVIA NARINS, and O'CONNOR, PATRICIA. *Le Français: Parler et Lire.* New York: Holt, Rinehart and Winston, Inc., 1963.
Second level materials which follow *Ecouter et Parler.* Introduction of reading as a source for conversation and pattern practice.

MAINOUS, BRUCE H. *Basic French: An Oral Approach.* New York: Charles Scribner's Sons, 1961.
Audio-lingual, conversation centered approach supplemented by pronunciation drills.

MALECOT, ANDRÉ. *Fundamental French: Language and Culture with Pattern Drills and Laboratory Exercises.* New York: Appleton-Century-Crofts, 1963.
Thirty lessons, each of which is developed on the basis of audio-visual cues derived in part from a photograph. Extensive laboratory drills of the transformation type.

MAUGER, G., and GOUGENHEIM, G. *Le Français élémentaire.* Paris: Librairie Hachette, 1957.
Lessons are based on dialogues illustrated by pictures. Pattern practice is integrated with a direct method approach.

MAUGER, G., *et al. Cours de langue et de civilisation française.* Paris: Librairie Hachette, 1958–64.
Complete sequence from elementary level to civilization text, using the direct method and a carefully planned progression of grammatical structures.

MARTY, FERNAND. *Spoken and Written French for the Language Laboratory, Book One and Book Two.* Wellesley, Massachusetts: Audio-Visual Publications, second edition, 1958.
A French grammar built on structural principles. French structure is presented primarily through transformation exercises. There is a time lag between the initial aural-oral presentation of the material and the student's familiarization with French orthography.

MORTON, F. RAND, and MUELLER, THEODORE, *et al. Experimental Self-Instructional Programmed Course in Contemporary Spoken French, Pre-Program "Prime."* Ann Arbor: The University of Michigan, Project AALP: II, 1963.
Student workbooks, magnetic tape recordings and script for an experimental audio-lingual self-instructional "programmed" course.

MUELLER, THEODORE. *La France et les Français.* Gainesville: Department of Foreign Languages, University of Florida, 1959.
Based on similar principles as in the *Images de France* mentioned above. The substitution technique is utilized in the exercise materials. The constructions and vocabulary included in the text take into consideration recommendations of the *Français élémentaire* study.

———. *La Structure de la langue française.* Detroit: Wayne State University, Audio-Visual Utilization Center, 1960.
Recorded drills with transcription covering most common structures and minimum vocabulary.

O'BRIEN, KATHRYN L., and LAFRANCE, MARIE STELLA. *New First-Year French.* Boston: Ginn and Co., 1958. *New Second-Year French.* Boston: Ginn and Co., 1958.

Typical for the adaptation of a "traditional" textbook to an audio-lingual approach through the addition of tapes and pattern practice type exercises.

POLITZER, ROBERT L. *Reading French Fluently.* A Structural Reading Approach to French. Englewood Cliffs, N.J.: Prentice-Hall, Inc., 1964.
A combined grammar and reader for the mature adult student who wants to acquire a reading knowledge of French as rapidly as possible. The principles of pattern practice, step learning, and structural recombination are utilized throughout the book.

POLITZER, ROBERT L., and HAGIWARA, M. P. *Active Review of French: Selected Patterns, Vocabulary and Pronunciation Problems for Speakers of English.* Boston: Ginn and Company, 1963.
Review of grammar for second year college, or third or fourth year high school. Spoken and written exercises utilizing transformation, substitution and cueing in English for pattern practice.

POLITZER, ROBERT L., HAGIWARA, MICHIO P., and CARDUNER, JEAN. *L'Echelle, structures essentielles du français.* New York: Blaisdell Publishing Co., 1965.
French grammar is presented in 220 learning steps, each utilizing pattern practice as well as written exercises. Conversational application of the pattern is stressed in review lessons and follows rather than precedes the drill of the pattern. Pictorial cues are utilized for the pattern drills, especially in the initial stages.

POLITZER, ROBERT L., and MARTINET, JEANNE. *Retour en France.* New York: American Book Company, 1964.
A reader for the "second level" (second or third year high school, second or third semester college) in which the pattern practice principle is applied to the development of reading skills and in which reading is integrated with audio-lingual exercises.

RICHARDS, I. A., ILSLEY, M. H., and GIBSON, CHRISTINE. *French Through Pictures.* New York: Cardinal Edition, Pocket Books Inc., 12th printing, 1959.
This book applies the simplification approach of "basic" English to the teaching of French. The structures which are "basic" (from the semantic point of view) are illustrated by stick figures which act out the "sense situation" from which the structures derive their meaning.

SEIBERT, L. C., and CROCKER, L. G. *Skills and Techniques for Reading French.* Baltimore: John Hopkins Press, 1958.
Structural analysis is applied to the problem of teaching reading. An entire section of the book is devoted to the recognition of word families and derivational endings.

STACK, EDWARD M. *Elementary Oral and Written French.* New York: Oxford University Press, 1959.
This book is based on the recommendations of the *Français élémentaire* study. Pattern practice is one of the main types of exercises used throughout.

STARR, WILMARTH H., and PELLEGRINO, ALFRED G. *New Functional French.* New York: American Book Co., 1959.
Pattern practice based on model sentences is one of the main pedagogical techniques used.

THOMPSON, MARY, *et al. A-LM*. *Audio-Lingual Materials: Listening, Speaking, Reading, Writing*. *French Level One*. New York: Harcourt, Brace and World, Inc., 1961. *French Level Two*. New York: Harcourt, Brace and World, Inc., 1962. *French Level Three*. In press.
Complete series of audio-lingual materials for junior high school and high school utilizing conversations, structural recomposition of essential elements, pattern practice. Tapes, records for the pupils, tests, teacher editions, teachers' manual, et cetera, are available.

Journals Dealing Primarily with Pedagogical Problems

Le Français dans le Monde (Revue de l'enseignement du français hors de France), Librairies Hachette et Larousse, Paris.
The French Review. American Association of Teachers of French, Eastern Michigan University, Ypsilanti, Mich.
Language Learning: A Journal of Applied Linguistics. English Language Institute, The University of Michigan, Ann Arbor, Michigan.
The Linguistic Reporter (Newsletter of the Center for Applied Linguistics), 1346 Connecticut Ave. N.W., Washington, D.C.
International Review of Applied Linguistics in Language Teaching. Julius Groos Verlag, Heidelberg, Germany.
ML Abstracts. Department of Foreign Languages and Literatures, Orange State College, Fullerton, California (Summaries of pedagogical research, methodological articles, et cetera).
The Modern Language Journal. National Federation of Modern Language Teachers Associations, St. Louis, Missouri.